DEAD RECKONINGS

A Review of Horror and the Weird in the Arts
Edited by Alex Houstoun and Michael J. Abolafia

No. 34 (Fall 2023)

- 3 A Weird Gourmand's Delight .... Daniel Pietersen
  Zara-Louise Stubbs, ed., *The Uncanny Gastronomic: Strange Tales of the Edible Weird*.

- 7 The Subtle Aroma of Antiquity: Two Translations by Shawn Garrett .... Karen Joan Kohoutek
  Jean Printemps, *Whimsical Tales* and Froylan Turcios, *The Vampire*; both tr. Shawn Garrett.

- 11 Night's Black Promises .... Géza A. G. Reilly
  Daniel Corrick, ed., *Night's Black Agents: An Anthology of Vampire Fiction*.

- 15 Nightlands Festival, Hammonton, NJ: Kathedral Event Center 2–3 June 2023 .... The joey Zone

- 19 Humor at Its Darkest .... Darrell Schweitzer
  Pablo Larrain, dir., *El Conde*.

- 21 Ramsey's Rant: Watch Their Language .... Ramsey Campbell

- 27 Wonder and Epiphany: The Question of Evil in the Stories of Arthur Machen .... Katherine Kerestman
  Arthur Machen, *Collected Fiction*, ed. by S. T. Joshi.

- 33 A New Lovecraftian Writer in Our Midst ..... Michael D. Miller
  Tony LaMalfa, *Forbidden Knowledge*.

- 38 Half Sunk a Shattered Visage Lies .... Daniel Pietersen
  Henry Bartholomew, ed., *The Living Stone: Stories of Uncanny Sculpture, 1858–1943*.

- 42 Covid Horrors .... S. T. Joshi
  Ramsey Campbell, *The Lonely Lands*.

- 46 Hungry .... Taylor Trabulus

- 50 Cultists Descend upon Portland: The H. P. Lovecraft Film Festival .... Katherine Kerestman

- 57 An Interview with Ellen Datlow .... Darrell Schweitzer

84 Sacred Scares .... Géza A. G. Reilly
Fiona Snailham, ed., *Holy Ghosts: Classic Tales of the Ecclesiastical Uncanny*.

87 Crossing the Void ....Michael D. Miller
Matt Cardin, *Journals, Volume 2: 2002–2022*.

95 New Ways to Dread the Holidays ....Dave Felton
Ellen Datlow, ed., *Christmas and Other Horrors: A Winter Solstice Anthology*.

99 About the Contributors

DEAD RECKONINGS is published by Hippocampus Press, P.O. Box 641, New York, NY 10156 (www.hippocampuspress.com). Copyright © 2024 by Hippocampus Press. Cover art by Jason C. Eckhardt. Cover design by Barbara Briggs Silbert. Hippocampus Press logo by Anastasia Damianakos. Orders and subscriptions should be sent to Hippocampus Press. Contact Alex Houstoun at deadreckoningsjournal@gmail.com for assignments or before submitting a publication for review.

ISSN 1935-6110   ISBN 9781614984276

A Weird Gourmand's Delight

Daniel Pietersen

ZARA-LOUISE STUBBS, ed. *The Uncanny Gastronomic: Strange Tales of the Edible Weird*. London: British Library, 2023. 286 pp. $15.99, £9.99 tpb. ISBN 9780712354288.

Food is strange. It shouldn't be, but it is. What appears at first to be everyday and mundane—quite literally of-the-earth—starts to take on an eerie flavor when we let our tongue linger in its folds and along its grain, when we savor it for slightly too long. Food isn't just fuel or building material for the body, but is an inanimate Other that becomes, through processes many of us don't fully understand if we even think of them at all, the animate Self. The unfamiliar becomes familiar—and what is more familiar to us than ourselves?—through machinery that is itself unfamiliar; a strange oscillation of Freud's concept of the Uncanny. Eating food, as editor Zara-Louise Stubbs explains in her introduction to this anthology, also summons up the ancient horror of *being eaten as food*, a concern we rarely allow to those creatures we ourselves feed upon. This quickly, as Stubbs states, "transcends the borders of the solely biological to enter the philosophical arena"; who can eat, what can they eat, and when can they eat it? What do we even consider edible and what do we think of those who disagree with us on that point? Food and feeding is bound up inextricably with what it is to be us; not just physically but politically, ethically, and even emotionally.

"We are what we eat" is far more accurate than it may at first seem.

Yes, reader, food is strange and no stranger than in the pages of *The Uncanny Gastronomic*, where cannibals rub shoulders with werewolves and gluttons are scowled at by abstainers. Here we find food that delights, food that disgusts, and food that does neither but disappoints in its bland indifference. Stubbs has curated a menu that contains not only all these varied dishes but also the diners, and the dined-upon, who hover over them, lips wet with anticipation. The mad, the bad, and the dangerous to gnaw . . .

It is difficult to pick favorites in this cornucopia as, like the best of menus, each relies on and contrasts with the others to offer up their full flavor. That said, "A Madman's Diary," written in the early years of the twentieth century by the Chinese writer Lu Xun, is an immediate stand-out; we follow the increasingly disorientated diary entries of an unnamed narrator—"I don't know whether it's day or night," he admits—as he becomes convinced that he lives in a village of cannibals. Worse than cannibals, in fact. His exclamation that "they only eat dead flesh" and his description of the villagers as "green faced, long toothed" marks them out as ghouls, carrion feeders. Although he appears to have no material evidence for his beliefs, whispered asides, "words between the lines," and his belief that "in ancient times, as I recollect, people often ate human beings" are enough to cement the idea in his mind. Yet it is the narrator himself who repeatedly obsesses over the eating of human flesh and who asks, "Is it right to eat human beings?" It is the narrator who has not seen the moon for thirty years, having been kept "in the dark" for all that time. We have to wonder whether the narrator of "A Madman's Diary" is entirely reliable or, as in Mark Twain's "Cannibalism in the Cars" (also included here), the fear of being eaten and the desire to eat has somehow become entwined in his "confused and incoherent" mind. It is a strange, haunting tale that rests uneasily in the reader's mind, as uneasily as the steamed fish— its mouth open "just like those people who want to eat human beings"—rests on the narrator's tongue.

In the introduction to "The Measure of My Powers" Stubbs tells us that the author, American food writer M. F. K. Fisher, stated that she wrote about food because "like most other humans, I am hungry." Yet, insightfully, Stubbs then asks whether this is a way of "querying what it is to be hungry." Hunger, even when it is still bound up with food, comes in many different forms; there can even be, in the overly pious, a hunger for hunger. In Fisher's anecdote, where the boundary between fiction and memoir feels slightly blurred, she tells of the conflict between Ora, a family cook who "loved to cook," and Fisher's grandmother, a stern and ascetic woman who "lived on rice-water and tomatoes stewed with white bread." Yet "The Measure of My Powers" is not just about food—not even when it is "exciting and new and delightful"—but about the preparation of food and the workings of the kitchen. The girl Fisher remembers herself as lingers in the kitchen that Ora has made her own, learning about herbs and meat and carrots in thin curls. Yet, more so even than these things, Fisher admits that "it is plain that most of my observations were connected in some way with Ora's knife." A curved knife, a French knife, a wicked knife. Fisher manages to take a domestic narrative, one filled with coziness and conflict as all homes are, and fold into it something sharp and bitter. This is a slice of life with an acidic, citric kick at the end.

My favorite piece in this collection, however, is Roald Dahl's "Pig." Although known for his children's stories—which Stubbs points out often include gastronomic themes such as unusual chocolates, gigantic fruit, and marvelous medicines—Dahl's wider body of short fiction consisted of strange tales of a more adult nature, many of which were adapted into the British television series *Tales of the Unexpected* (1979–88). In "Pig," the strange and gleeful cruelty that could be considered Dahl's trademark abounds, but here it is targeted more at the reader than the characters. Lexington, the tale's protagonist, bounds from death to death to death with an optimism and rapidity that would be worthy of Voltaire's *Candide*. Indeed, the link between the two is made overt by Dahl's use of Glosspan as the name of Lexington's unexpectedly kindly great aunt, reversing the Pangloss of Candide's tutor. Lexington, raised as a vegetarian by his aunt, expresses bewildered surprise when he learns that "ordinary people" eat meat, which he only vaguely understands comes from animals. He absorbs the information, however, as he has absorbed everything his aunt teaches him and is even more bewildered when he inadvertently eats meat, albeit perhaps not meat from animals, and finds it to be delicious. The result of this discovery is as knife-quick and unpleasantly savage as Dahl himself could be.

The success of *The Uncanny Gastronomic*, however, lies not

so much in its individual tales as in the atmosphere conjured by the breadth of entries Stubbs has blended together. We move from horror anthology stalwarts such as Algernon Blackwood, Edgar Allan Poe, and Angela Carter through Franz Kafka's liminal worlds and then on to ostensibly "literary" writers such as Virginia Woolf and Italo Calvino. It is a bold recipe, yet one that allows the reader to explore different variations of the weird tale—the horrifying, the unsettling, the disgusting—just as each writer's characters explore different examples of food and feeding and being fed upon. The weird, Stubbs seems to imply, is not just those inexplicable things that creep from abyssal voids but is also the everyday, domestic world placed under such microscopic inspection that it starts to bubble and boil and froth.

The Uncanny Gastronomic shows us that while food is indeed strange, it is only so because it exists in—and is necessary to—a deeply strange world, inhabited by deeply strange beings. Food, in fact, is strange because everything is strange.

The Subtle Aroma of Antiquity: Two Translations by Shawn Garrett

Karen Joan Kohoutek

JEAN PRINTEMPS. *Whimsical Tales*. Translated by Shawn Garrett. N.p.: Snuggly Books, 2022. 194 pp. $16.50 tpb. ISBN: 9781645250944.

FROYLÁN TURCIOS. *The Vampire*. Translated by Shawn Garrett. N.p.: Strange Ports Press, 2023. 170 pp. $23.24 hc. ISBN: 9798987681091. $16.24 tpb. ISBN: 9798987681084.

> Within a century, there will hardly be a faint memory of us. Who, then, will pronounce our names?—Froylán Turcios, *The Vampire*

Shawn M. Garrett, an editor with the *Pseudopod* podcast and a former editor of short fiction at Wildside Press (from whom I bought many books in the early 2000s), has been hard at work translating obscure literary works, most recently published through Garrett's own Strange Ports Press. These are mostly examples of Decadent literature, a late nineteenth-century aesthetic movement focused on excess, sensuality, and "art for art's sake." *Whimsical Tales*, written by Jean Printemps (1885), and Froylán Turcios's *The Vampire* (1910) both serve as intriguing introductions to Garrett's output. While they may not exactly be weird tales, they're certainly curious ones.

Whimsical Tales is written in a style that doesn't get much public notice; it is made up of short, sometimes cryptic stories, not bound to realism in any way, often reading like fairy tales with philosophical or satirical intent. I was reminded of Horace Walpole's peculiar *Hieroglyphic Tales*, but there is also some resemblance to more contemporary surrealists such as Djuna Barnes.

The book's back cover calls the short stories "droll," which is an apt description. Many of them involve the justice system or the military and share several common concerns. The first two stories are about how idealism can be carried too far, to the point where those attempting to reach their ideals are driven mad. Several stories deal with injustice and the capriciousness of authority, like the judge who believes that "Society was a kind of deity to whom human sacrifices were needed."

Other human foibles are addressed, such as the boy in "A Child's Tale." He is never satisfied with his current state, metamorphosing into various forms, finding, for example, that "it seemed fun to be inert matter." The boy inevitably tires of that too, until he finally learns a lesson about appreciating what he has. Another story proves that the trope of the "snipe hunt" as an initiation ritual is one that goes back to at least the 1880s (here called a "guer-houp," or "war whoop").

Touches of metafiction also appear, as when Printemps refers to a character "whom you could have known if she existed elsewhere than in the imagination of the author of this true story!" The most striking story may be "The Battle of the Dead," in which the skeletons of dead soldiers come to life to re-fight their old conflicts, even though, as one of them says, "it bores me a lot." It's a good example of Printemps's mix of light-hearted satire with the harshness of existence.

The book looks good, with a colorful cover and professional formatting, which I don't take for granted from small presses. Information on the publisher's website states that Printemps's work appeared in a journal called *La Lanterne*, "but aside from that, very little is known about him." That is an obstacle, but I would have been grateful for any contextualization possible. Even the publication date of 1885 is only referenced on the back cover and in the "about the author' section, not in the text itself. I am even assuming, but not absolutely certain, that Printemps was French, having been fooled by the Belgian Hercule Poirot in my youth.

The short novel *The Vampire* (*El Vampiro)* has a very different tone. Written by Froylán Turcios, a noted Honduran author and influential journalist, it is a fresh addition to the canon of Decadent literature. The protagonist and his love interest live an emotionally overheated, claustrophobic life, isolating themselves in a shared life of the mind. They are dragged to social events, where they only want to discuss art and aesthetics with each other. With a dark family secret and a classically Gothic sinister priest in the background, it is inevitable that real trouble will befall these dreamy idealists.

Many aspects of their story could be placed in a classically Gothic European manor, but while young Rogerio and his beloved cousin Luz are enamored of continental literary works, especially the Germans (along with the American Edgar Allan Poe, of course), their story takes place in the aristocratic society of Guatemala, transporting the tropes of Romanticism to a new setting.

Turcios shows the characters' sensibility as overwrought, even pretentious; Rogerio scorns the "perfumed frivolity" of Paris and describes his beloved as "a true enchanting oasis in that sterile desert of feminine mental ineptitude." At the same time, I suspect that Turcios was, at times, using them as mouthpieces for his own beliefs.

For example, the novel contains some lengthy rants against development. Luz says that "houses of modern style" will soon be built, and future visitors "will be indignant at our criminal disdain for the legacies of the centuries." Faced with progress that will devastate the landscape and lead to a generic modernization, young Rogerio argues that it will only benefit the already wealthy, not the region's poor, and that the area's value as a tourist destination is based on antiquity, and the unique character that will be lost in becoming "a commercial town like any of the other commercial towns that by the hundreds fill the world." This objection is met with an accusation that "all that is romanticism, dreams, ideations, vague longings. Air castles, legends, boulders; everything that is useless wind and vagueness will have to disappear amid the deafening noises of locomotives and factories." Some things never change.

The story is thin, as mysterious plot threads are forgotten for lengthy periods, only to recur when least expected. That leaves the supernatural side of the story unfortunately underdeveloped. But the lush language weaves a spell, and the philosophical digressions, as sampled above, are interesting, often more than the romance.

There are some formatting issues in this edition that may be a problem for readers. The text is printed blog-style, with a line between each block paragraph, which cries out "self-published" in a negative way, as do the inconsistent font sizes. The table of contents uses a tiny font for the chapter headings (just "Chapter XXVI," for example), a larger font with bold-face chapter headings in the text, then a third, medium-sized font for the listing of other Strange Ports Press books. I got used to these elements, but I did find them off-putting, and together they add up to a book that doesn't look unprofessional.

Garrett includes an afterword discussing the novel's themes and storyline, but again there is little context about the author or the work. In this case, I am assuming from the title *El Vampiro* that it was translated from Spanish. For both these books, I would have been grateful for more background. How did Garrett even come across these works? What sources did he use as the base for the translations? These aren't scholarly editions, and I know many people may scoff at academics, but this would be useful information for anyone who is intrigued by the artists or time period and would like to learn more.

Still, as far as I can tell, these are the only English translations of either writer that exist, unless they are hidden in collections that don't list their contents in online records. *The Vampire* is possibly the only example of Honduran Decadent writing in print in English. This alone makes these publications valuable additions to our store of knowledge about the literature of the past. It seems self-evident that both these books have a niche appeal. But they are both short, you are unlikely to get bogged down in the language, and they open up an interesting literary space in time. So despite the fussiness I learned from my old English professors, both these books, and the other productions of Snuggly Books and Strange Ports Press, are well worth checking out.

Night's Black Promises

Géza A. G. Reilly

DANIEL CORRICK, ed. *Night's Black Agents: An Anthology of Vampire Fiction*. N.p.: Snuggly Books, 2023. 270 pp. $21.00 tpb. ISBN: 9781645251316.

Night's Black Agents is a solid anthology. I enjoyed reading it, and I think that if others are, like me, fans of slightly antiquated vampire fiction, then I suspect that they will too. Really, there isn't a stinker of a tale here, and they have all been grouped together by an editor who clearly loves and is intellectually invested in this material. However, I must admit that I was nevertheless left a bit cold by my experience of *Night's Black Agents*. I believe that is because, at the end of the day, an anthology of vampire fiction is all that *Night's Black Agents* is.

That is disappointing to me because the introduction to the anthology, provided by the delightfully astute Daniel Corrick, promises so much more. Indeed, I think it isn't going too far to say that the introduction is the best part of *Night's Black Agents*. Corrick provides the reader with a concise and engaging history of the literary vampire and the meaning with which that symbol has been imbued by a variety of societal groups over the years. For example, I was thrilled to read Corrick's insights into how the vampire was a figure balanced on a knife's edge between being a representation of libidinal libertine desire on the one hand and the vile indulgences of the upper classes on the other. Reading Corrick delve briefly into the vampire's ties to spirituality was a breath of fresh air, too, particularly in the pains he took to make it clear that one does not need to subscribe to a religion to see why the flaunting of that faith could disturb readers. Corrick's introduction made me excited to read the stories that followed, and as someone who has read a good many introductions to scholarly texts, that is a rarity to be treasured.

Yet I found that the stories in *Night's Black Agents* didn't quite follow the trajectory that Garrick had laid out for me. Sure, there are horrendous members of the gentry haunting some of these pages, and there certainly are libidinal desires here and there, but I never got the sense that everything was gelling together into a curated, cohesive whole. Rather, I was left feeling as though Corrick's introduction was describing some *other* set of tales rather than the ones I had on hand. I am not sure if that's unfair of me, but I think it is reasonable to assume that the introduction of a volume will accurately reflect the rest of the contents of that volume. And with an introduction as strong as Corrick's, a cohesive, strong theme should be present in every entry on the table of contents.

I recognize, however, that sometimes a good anthology of vampire fiction—of *whatever* kind—is all a reader needs to get them through, and such a person certainly shouldn't be disappointed by what *is* on offer in *Night's Black Agents*. Focusing almost exclusively on the vampires of the nineteenth century, the anthology begins with a fairly predictable selection in "The Vampyre" by John Polidori, but it quickly rockets off into numerous tales that I frankly had never heard of before. I was particularly gripped by "The Bruxa" by William Kingston, which *is* one of the stories that focuses on the spiritual metaphor bound up in the figure of the vampire. And I was equally enthralled by Alexander Dumas's "The Pale Lady," which, in addition to possessing all that symbolic frippery, also happens to be a rollicking tragic adventure story (should anyone expect otherwise from Dumas?). Even the clunkiest of stories, "The Vampyre Bride" by Edwin Roberts, is only clunky in the sense that it is a retelling of some aspects of the historical Countess Báthori Erzsébet—not in the sense of the story's merit in terms of its style or presentation.

Out of the thirteen stories in *Night's Black Agents*, only four date to the twentieth century for their composition. It is interesting to see how the vampire has dropped even more of the libertine, upper crust, and religious overtones Carrick set out in his introduction in this period. The latest tale on offer, "Doctor Horder's Room" by Patrick Carleton, dates to 1935, and while it is a fun read, it falls a bit flat by coming across more as an example of boy's-first-occult-detective material than anything else. Still, "Our Lady of Red Lips" (1910) by Aimée Crocker is a fascinating prose-poem seemingly intended to create a vampire narrative out of the most minimal of components, and "The Vampire" (1918) by Leonhard Stein is a wonderful take on the evolution of the vampire—with its blasphemous nature taken from the health of the soul and applied instead to one's ability to produce at work. I personally would be interested in seeing an anthology that specifically traces the evolution of the vampire over the decades and centuries—and if it is introduced by Daniel Corrick, then all the better.

Overall, *Night's Black Agents* is a worthy read for vampire fans. I do fear, however, that it is just another anthology of vampire fiction. The overall quality of the stories makes it a standout, perhaps, but I am not sure whether that alone is sufficient to make the anthology worthy of collection on our shelves. Perhaps I am being overly picky, but I truly feel that the stories collected here do not live up to the high bar set by the introduction, which is, I fully admit, an unusual thing to say—let alone an unusual standard by which to review a book. Allow me to end, then, by saying that the vampire is a figure that many have argued has been drained of its power due to overfamiliarity. *Night's Black Agents* suggests that we might still find life in those horrible corpses, but the stories, particularly in their historical distance, do not quite allow us to find that vitality for ourselves. Rather, like a well-written eulogy at a funeral, they serve more to remind us of how vibrant that figure *used* to be for other people. Delight in these stories, then, but do not be surprised if, like me, you come away thinking that this anthology could have been just a little bit more.

Artwork by Josh Yelle

Nightlands Festival, Hammonton, NJ: Kathedral Event Center 2–3 June 2023

The joey Zone

The Nightlands Festival was one of the most singular events ever attended—an artistic quest through darkened sonic spheres only navigated by that surest vehicle—which is the single human voice. The dream of Jonathan Dennison, this "Celebration of Literary Nightmares" ran just one weekend this past summer. Dennison is the founder of Cadabra Records, an imprint of Spoken Art founded in 2015, an amalgam incorporating soundscapes with art and scholarship to complete each vinyl artifact. Held at The Kathedral Event Center—which operated as a Catholic church in a previous incarnation—the mid-century architecture was witness to a truly different sort of religious experience.

An Artists Alley reminiscent of the best pre-2013 NecronomiCons included Dave Felton, Matthew Jaffe, Jeremy Hush (purveying copies of *Ekphrastic Beasts*, a creature compendium for gamers which he contributed to), Paul Romano, and Josh Yelle. Also vending was Matt Bartlett (whose work was performed in a pre-show reading midweek) and Mike "My Middle Name is HORROR" Hunchback (editor of *Pulp Macabre*). Hippocampus had two tables of books. There were festival exclusives available from Cadabra and its publishing extension Chiroptera Press. Fittingly, a chapbook was created to mark the proceedings by Felton—"The Festival"—which was put into hands gratis of that inestimable illuminator.

The introduction of S. T. Joshi to the crowd opened the festivities. His presence alone was reason to attend this weekend, as it has been far too long since he was a listed participant in any convention on the East Coast. Joshi gave a verbal foreword to the first spoken word performance, that being M. R. James's "Count Magnus." With a projection of Matt Jaffe's painting for the Cadabra release (CADABR-91 [2022]) behind him, Robert Lloyd Parry, arguably THE James impersonator, gave a nuanced reading of "Magnus," with any pauses and occasional silences in his delivery only adding to a perfect whole.

Fig 1: Also available at the Festival were remaining copies of Dave Felton's chapbook for an earlier performance of "The Clown Puppet." Portrayed in this panel is Chris Bozzone (upper left), Padgett (upper right) and Cadabra's master of puppets himself, Jonathan Dennison (lower center).

Next up was Jon Padgett delivering Thomas Ligotti's "The Clown Puppet," to these eyes apparently from memory (CADABR-86 [2022]). Jon (a.k.a. Dr. Locrian), a veritable Ligottian Evangelist, was a revelation himself. If you ever have a chance to attend one of his initially-hilarious-cum-insidiously-harrowing interpretations, do so with no hesitation. British character actor Lawrence R. Harvey followed with his fine rendition of "The Human Chair" by Edogawa Rampo (a Japanese writer whose name is a takeoff from Poe) (CADABR-20 [2018]), accompanied by Slasher Film Strategy. His voice cut through the shadowed rafters of Kathedral like a knife out of a sheath.

After that was the first of the two panels scheduled in the Festival, this initial conversation being on "The Craft Behind Cadabra." This writer did cameo interviews with Padgett, Harvey, Jonathan Dennison, and the next performer on deck, Andrew Leman of the H. P. Lovecraft Historical Society. They all described the process involved in creating each Cadabra product, starting with Dennison and how he chooses which particular voice to go with each record, followed by the other panelists describing their initiation to the label.

Andrew concluded Friday's schedule with a presentation of "The Lurking Fear" (CADABR-005 [2016]), giving a haunted account from the very first paragraphs. Even after the end of the first day, this reviewer remained gripped, enraptured, yet I was not alone, for foolhardiness was not then mixed with that love of the grotesque and the terrible which has made my career a series of quests for strange horrors in literature and in life.

Mention must be made of Chris Bozzone, a soundtrack composer who started working with Cadabra in 2017. His contributions to our group pilgrimage provided the cohesiveness to the entire weekend's aesthetic.

A repeat of Friday's lineup doing equally strong material was the only way Day Two of the Festival could compare. Our love of horror and literature did not go unrequited! In some cases, performances even surpassed in intensity. Lloyd Parry's reading of Cadabra's upcoming release of Algernon Blackwood's "The Willows" held one increasingly spellbound up to that last cadence of "turning over and over on the waves like an otter." Jon Padgett effortlessly managed another star turn with "Mrs. Rinaldi's Angel" (CADABR-97 [2022]). Laurence Harvey previewed an upcoming label release that includes Baudelaire's "Litanies to Satan" (one of the high points of the festival). Credit Where Due was paid in the second panel, "The Art of Cadabra Records," including Felton, Jaffe, Yelle, Hush, and Romano with additional teasers for a Cadabra release of "The Rats in the Walls" (a 4-LP boxset!) and Chiroptera Press publications of Thomas Ligotti's *Noctuary* and *Crampton,* with art by Paul Romano and Dave Felton respectively. Andrew Leman brought us all home at the end of the night—to Dunwich, that is.

If the idea of sitting through two days of Spoken Word is still hard for you to visualize, let me accentuate: it just *sang*. This choir in the Kathedral—voices in performance and the response of attendees, all testifying to The Weird Aesthetic as one—made visible that dream that we will hopefully wake to again somewhere in years to come.

Fig 2: Artists of Cadabra from left to right: Jeremy Hush, Matthew Jaffe, Josh Yelle "Pencilmancer," Paul Romano, and Dave Felton (Photo courtesy of Dave Felton's phone)

Humor at Its Darkest

Darrell Schweitzer

El Conde. Fabula, 2023. Chilean film directed by Pablo Larrain. Starring Jaime Vadell, Gloria Műnchmeyer, Alfredo Castro, Paula Luchsinger. 110 Minutes. In Spanish, but available dubbed in English on Netflix.

The most memorable image in the Chilean film *El Conde* (The Count) is that of a man in military uniform and cloak soaring serenely over a modern city, the cloak flapping in the wind. With black-and-white photography and a slightly soft focus, this could well be a shot from some art-house foreign film of the 1950s, perhaps early Fellini. But it is not. The flying man is a vampire. He lands, enters the apartment of a female victim, slits her throat with a curved knife he carries, then extracts her still-beating heart, flies home (to a remote farm) with it, liquefies it in a blender, and drinks it.

Is this a horror film? Is it black comedy? Actually, I think, it will take a considerable leap of imagination for American viewers to grasp what *El Conde* must mean to a Chilean audience, because its basic premise is that the allegedly dead dictator Augusto Pinochet is really a 250-year-old vampire, very much still with us, although he is losing his zest for his predatory existence and has been eating only vegetables of late. Those aerial, vampiric raids are actually the work of his White Russian sidekick Fyodor, also a vampire, who wears Pinochet's uniform, perhaps to give the impression that the Count is up to his old tricks.

This is political satire, its humor so dark that, as a Ukrainian friend of mine remarked about the similarly satirical *The Death of Stalin* (2017), you're going to need a flashlight. Imagine such a film about, say, Saddam Hussein, Idi Amin, or, once the world is rid of him, Vladimir Putin, made within living memory of his tyranny, viewed by an audience who suffered under his regime, many of them relatives of people who "disappeared." In real life Pinochet took power in 1973 in the CIA-greenlighted coup that resulted in the death of Chile's elected socialist president Salvador Allende. Torture, massacres, and a reign of terror followed, while US presidents disgracefully received him as a client and ally. He made himself vastly rich in office. He was forced to step down in 1990 after losing a plebiscite and the support of his junta, though he remained head of the Chilean army until 1998, when he retired to become senator for life and apparently thought himself free from prosecution. He was arrested in London for human rights violations and embezzlement on an international warrant, but his close friend Margaret Thatcher sent him back to Chile. He was facing multiple charges when he finally died in 2006.

Or did he? There's the joke. We see a very real picture of Pinochet in his coffin at his funeral, but his eyes move and there is briefly a sly look on his face. Subsequently Fyodor's nightly depredations convince Pinochet's five adult, ne'er-do-well children that he will never really die and they will never get their inheritance, which is hidden in foreign bank accounts. They hire Carmen, a nun, to pretend to be an accountant to go over the books at Pinochet's farm, but actually to exorcise and kill him. Things do not go as planned. There are twists and surprises, which I will not spoil for you. An equally undead Mrs. Thatcher shows up to complicate matters. Everybody scrambles for the loot. Pinochet regains his zest for existence and avails himself of some of the frozen human hearts kept in the basement.

For Americans, this all will probably seem a bit remote. We never feared and hated this monster. We cannot feel the release Chileans must be able to feel seeing him transformed into a comic grotesque. It would be as if the Germans, a generation after World War II, made *The Great Dictator,* only they crossed it with *Dracula*. For us the film hovers somewhere between a curio and exotic foreign art. Not your usual vampire film, certainly.

Ramsey's Rant: Watch Their Language

Ramsey Campbell

One reason I regard the best horror fiction as literature is that it generally achieves its effects through the choice of language: the precise selection and arrangement of words, the modulation of prose, the rhythm and music of the text. In my experience, no writer in the field cared more about these elements than Lovecraft did, not just in his own work but in his critical essays (though the two aren't necessarily separable: a writer analysing other writers may often be discussing their own work or their intentions for it by proxy, and *Supernatural Horror in Literature* frequently describes in terms of his ambitions for the field the works Lovecraft cites). Elsewhere I've scrutinised "The Rats in the Walls" in detail, finding that one of its themes is language itself and its range. I neglected to touch on the pet cat's infamous name, but that's relevant to my argument, given how the reader's experience inevitably reflects the prevailing change of attitude to such a use of the word. Yes, it's casually racist, but not maliciously intended, since it borrowed its name from Lovecraft's own pet, named well before he reached his teens and presumably endorsed if not chosen by his family. The adjective was still in common use in the sixties to describe a shade of dye, and this kind of use had yet to be classed as a racial slur, at least in my lived experience of the period (whereas I made my distaste plain when an uncle applied it to Martin Luther King). On the basis of all this I'd suggest that an inadvertent but crucial theme of Lovecraft's tale, especially given the death of the author in both the physical and the Barthesian sense, is the perception of language and how this perception mutates.

I leave this observation for what it may be worth and move on to the larger issue of the language of our field. As with so many aspects of the genre, Mary Shelley is seminal. "He held up the curtains of the bed, and his eyes, if eyes they may be called, were fixed on me." Is that questioning clause the first instance of words that suggest worse than they show? She refined the Gothic, giving voice to the monster, whose language demonstrates its capacity to learn and develop, though (unlike, say, "Flowers for Algernon") the prose style doesn't actively depict this progress. Poe takes distillation further, creating monologues that resemble texts for performance, though he appears never to have performed them. That said, the voice of mental disintegration hardly needs to be pronounced aloud when it can be heard so clearly on the page. In Britain, Le Fanu condenses the Gothic. While his prose is more deliberate than Poe's, they have in common an instinct for the accumulation of telling detail, celebrated by Lovecraft in Poe, hailed by M. R. James in Le Fanu.

Bierce explores the effect of assembling different voices in "The Moonlit Road," that occidental cousin of *Rashomon*, but what are we to make of "The Middle Toe of the Right Foot"? Can the effect of tailing the tale with a circumstantial but crucial piece of information rather than incorporating this within the body of the narrative really be evidence of structural carelessness and nothing else? Might it be intended to impart a kind of journalistic verisimilitude to the tale, mimicking the presentation of bare facts? Lovecraft thought the story clumsily developed and elsewhere criticised Algernon Blackwood's style as excessively journalistic, but is that approach necessarily second-rate? In Blackwood's case it enables him to scrutinise the psychological effect of the uncanny on his characters, and doesn't prevent him from gradually gathering a sense of dread or awe in his finest work.

Newspaperman Arthur Machen uses it to simulate authenticity in "The Great Return" and "The Bowmen" (in that case so convincingly that a cleric told him to his face he hadn't made the story up), but his greatest achievement is "The White People," that haunting use of the naïve voice. A child's viewpoint, with all its limitations and potential misperceptions, can intensify dread—see examples as varied as Richard Matheson's "Born of Man and Woman" and Villy Sørensen's "Child's Play"—and the lyrical innocence of the young girl's journal in Machen's tale transports us to the highest level of the adumbrated occult. It's also a classic case of the unaware narrator, a device especially suited to our field and perhaps the point where horror comes closest to tragedy, by allowing the audience to see or anticipate what the narrator can't. "August Heat," that perfect miniature, exemplifies the device.

Does this approach risk undermining the horror—letting the reader indulge in a complicit grin or smirk at the protagonist's imminent fate? Not in the Harvey tale, at least in my experience, but what of, say, Stanley Ellin's "The Speciality of the House," widely anthologised for horror? It's an elegantly witty piece, tipping the reader the wink about the situation with a single adjective in the final line. We find Lovecraft using a similar adjective in "The Rats in the Walls," where it gains a baleful power from repetition, so that its initial innocent occurrence takes on retrospective significance. One difference may well be that in the Lovecraft tale it's just one element in the orchestration of the prose towards producing dread. Yet although in "The Two Bottles of Relish" Lord Dunsany is as reticent as Ellin on a comparably ghoulish theme, his coda conveys a shudder despite if not because of its restraint. Perhaps Ellin simply judged the level of explicitness the Ellery Queen magazine would accept, and offered its readers amusement but no more. Still, do we smile even grimly at the payoff of "The Man Who Liked Dickens," a tale equally delicate in its depiction? Crucial as language is, the vision it conveys must surely be as well, and Waugh's humour (here and in "Mr Loveday's Little Outing"), while as sly as Ellin's, is founded on a dark view of humanity and the world. Again, spareness of prose can bring a bleak chill (Hemingway's "The Killers") or epitomise enigma (almost anything by Aickman).

Horror fiction often resurrects and revitalises language. Lovecraft relished eloquent archaism, and revived Poe's prose in his own, as in a different way *Lolita* did. M. R. James delighted in pastiche, occasionally casting an entire tale in that form, and perhaps Lovecraft learned from or was at any rate encouraged by his example, traces of which I find in the *Necronomicon* quote in "The Dunwich Horror," for instance. James surely inspired Kingsley Amis to compose Underhill's journal in *The Green Man* (where the climactic manifestation of the titular entity heightens and compacts the style to express urgent terror). Can we see a recognisable influence in one of Cormac McCarthy's horror novels, *Outer Dark*? It contains not just "nameless" but "eldritch," while *Blood Meridian* in particular glories in restoring linguistic rarities. Pastiche is rampant in *The Highgate Vampire* and its siblings, lending a new sense to Gothic revival.

How effective a choice of words may be in a macabre tale (or indeed any other kind) must ultimately depend on the reader. Take the contents of the cupboards in Blackwood's "Chemical" and Onions' "The Beckoning Fair One." Blackwood's indirectness—his repetition of the single word "upright"—gives me an authentic chill, whereas Onions' use of "pudding" falls short of me, I fear (or rather, wish I feared). Repetition can add potency, though. Remember Marley's face.

Marley's face. Its recurrence, ending a paragraph and beginning its successor, is one source of the power of the image. I gather Louis Zukovsky argues that the way prose is set out on the page affects the reader's experience, and this is certainly the case (at least for me) with M. R. James. James was a master of distilling dread into a single glimpse that suggested even worse than it showed, and equally skilled at conveying horror by witty indirection—see Lord Robert's fate in "The Ash-Tree" for a grisly instance—but I believe another aspect of his prose is crucial: how it is presented to the reader. I'll cite the unfortunate Mr Dunning's search for matches in "Casting the Runes" as an instance. In the Edward Arnold editions and most others of James, the shock lies low in the middle of a paragraph, adding greatly to its power. A recent collection of James broke this passage into (count them) seven paragraphs, ruining the effect. It was argued that James wrote his tales for reading aloud and had little concern with how they appeared on the page. Yet presumably he saw these publications, and I have yet to see evidence that he disapproved of how they looked. Indeed, *The Five Jars* (written for publication) uses exactly the same style of paragraph.

At least the paragraphing is less offensive than the wholesale rewrite of "'Oh, Whistle and I'll Come to You, My Lad'" perpetrated by Michael Cox (not to be mistaken for a distinguished anthologist of the same name) in one of a pair of horrid vandalistic books aimed—indeed, hurled—at young folk, *Twisted Tales*. A more fruitful comparison can be made between James' "The Diary of Mr Poynter" and J. Paul Suter's "Beyond the Door" (admired by Lovecraft and Dashiell Hammett, among others). Suter's climactic scene reads like a vulgarisation of the James tale. Where James presents his spectral revelation in a single paragraph composed of suggestive details culminating in a monstrous glimpse followed by pursuit, Suter races through his set-piece in several short paragraphs that lead to a declarative sentence entirely in capitals, which do it and the scene no good. The contrast between the stories exemplifies the importance of another element: pacing. Along with timing, tempo and indeed rubato are as crucial to the effectiveness of a tale of terror as these qualities are to music. Adam Nevill has noted how James tends to use neutral language to depict his uncanny manifestations, a principle Nevill applies to his own powerful work.

Poe and Lovecraft favoured unity of effect in their tales of terror, but Lovecraft also championed documentary realism. Sometimes the former technique can overwhelm the latter. In the Suter story, is the police detective who succumbs to hysteria, having found a corpse—"He began to laugh—a little, high cackle, like a child's"—too much of a good Gothic thing? In particular Frank Belknap Long demonstrates the potential pitfalls of imposing too much unity on the narrative. Take "The Space-Eaters." Treating a Lovecraftian notion with the lyrical weirdness of Machen, parts of it are truly inspired (especially the long hand, a concept with which the author's surrogate impresses his friend Howard), but a commitment to unity flaws the tale. Since the pair of central characters write weird fiction, perhaps they can be allowed to speak as if they do, but when this proves true of a doctor and even a policeman, it reads as though the invading aliens have spread some semantic infection. Long's prose displays several distinct periods. Writing for *Unknown Worlds* appears to have moderated his approach while preserving his inventiveness, but the science fiction boom of the fifties may have proved less beneficial. Harlan Ellison complained that as an editor Long exemplified the perils payment by the word entailed, and too often this was true of Long the writer. At times his linguistic luxuriation borders on the experimental. Consider *The Night of the Wolf*. Towards the end of chapter three the narrator sees no vulture in the sky, which prompts him to speculate for three paragraphs what the situation would be like if there were one. In chapter nine two characters discuss in excruciating detail for an entire page whether someone might have gone into a wood, while later in the chapter they take more than a page to pick over what could have befallen a weasel, and even then the subject isn't exhausted, though the reader may be. Passages like these (and they are many) recall the obsessive permutations of activity Beckett's characters are wont to perform.

Since I can find no other slot for Beckett in these ruminations, I'll head for the coda by citing his horror novel *The Unnamable*, written in prose that barely takes a breath and demands to be read in a single sitting (which I did). Few fictions fit their form and their prose as closely, indeed obsessively, to their theme—in this case perhaps a nightmare vision of the afterlife—as this does. And I'll finish with an instance that that has horrified me as profoundly as any passage in fiction: the fate of Krug's son in *Bend Sinister*. Whereas in *Lolita* Nabokov renders murder dreadful by reinventing it as dark comedy, the atrocities in *Bend Sinister* are described in matter-of-fact clinical language, which makes them well-nigh unbearable. Should we conclude there are as many approaches to the question of depiction as there are inspired writers? I'm inspired to end that way, at any rate.

Wonder and Epiphany: The Question of Evil in the Stories of Arthur Machen

Katherine Kerestman

ARTHUR MACHEN. *Collected Fiction*. Edited by S. T. Joshi. New York: Hippocampus Press, 2019. 3 vols. 1645 pp. $90.00 tpb. ISBN: 9781614982852.

Reading the complete fiction of Arthur Machen for the first time, I was struck, not only by the surreal literary experience of reading Machen—the result of his dreamlike plots, fantastic settings, and melodious diction—but by the persistent presence of evil in Machen's dream worlds, two salient characteristics of his work. Fixing his gaze on the sorrows of the individual—personal misery that is caused by the evil intrinsic in human nature and institutions, and also by the evil that exists in the cosmos at large—Machen studies evil, attempting to discern its essence, although he never arrives at an explanation. Through such pleasing tropes as fairies and troglodytes, human/monster hybrids, witches and cults, and killer plants, Machen explores the evils of bullying, rape, lack of human sympathy, devastation of our shared natural resources, exploitation, war, murder, and sundry other narcissistic behaviors that cause grave injury to other people. His fantastic weird stories are characterized by dread, horror, terror, and disgust, and they burn so slowly that the tension increases bit by bit until the reader cannot bear to put the book down before he or she has come to the resolution of the horrific proposition of the plot. While this essay will primarily focus on three of my favorite stories, "The White People," *The Hill of Dreams,* and "A Fragment of Life," it is worth noting that from his earlier works, such as seminal novella "The Great God Pan" (1894), to those later in his life and career, such as "Scrooge and the Spirit of Psychoanalysis," Machen continued to explore these questions of evil and wonder.

"The Great God Pan" (1894), undeniably Machen's best-known work, is infamous for the devastation it wrought upon its struggling author's reputation at the time of publication. The story was denounced by the arbiters of taste and morality at the end of the nineteenth century as degenerate and perverse because of the suggested sexual content. It wasn't until the end of Machen's life that the novella was reconsidered and began to be considered a classic of the horror genre. Dr. Raymond of "The Great God Pan" sacrifices a loved one to satisfy his intellectual curiosity, causing the suffering and death of a young woman as well as the opening of a gateway through which cosmic evil enters the world.

"Scrooge and the Spirit of Psycho-Analysis," one of Machen's later, very short stories or vignettes, is a satire deriding the dogged determination of modern science to deprive people of their capacity for wonder—to tell us all that there is no Santa Claus. Wonder, in Machen, is the faculty that enables one to experience that which is outside and yet within oneself—to be fully alive. Wonder exists beyond the mundane business of material existence, and it comprises such phenomena as the consideration of other people's feelings (empathy) and awareness of the universe and humankind's relation to it (philosophy). In some of Machen's other tales, though, a greater awareness is fraught with danger.

My favorite stories are in *Collected Fiction, Volume 2: 1896–1910*: "The White People," *The Hill of Dreams,* and "A Fragment of Life." These stories have in common a setting in a prehistoric England of barrows and stone circles, fairies and trolls, and occasional human sacrifices. In "The White People," two men engaged in a dialogue about the nature of evil read the Green Book (the diary of a girl who is initiated by her nurse into a witch cult, a circumstance that occasions the early death of the maiden). *The Hill of Dreams* is the story of Lucian Taylor, whose dream life overtakes his real life, illustrating the danger of an uncontrolled wonder. Failing to keep one foot in the concrete, prosaic world, Lucian becomes consumed by his own dark pagan fantasies. *The Hill of Dreams* questions at which point the dream world—the realm of beauty, majesty, and magic—crosses the line into insanity; and it questions whether making the choice to dwell in the greater consciousness rather than the here and now is the same as madness. Furthermore, it begs the question whether insanity is necessarily inferior to a life bereft of imagination. Indulging in wonder may lead to terrible pain. Is the alternative worse?

Lovely, exquisite, magnificent, joyous, "A Fragment of Life," Machen's tender tale of the growth of love and compassion in the awakening of a married couple to a greater awareness deserves a more extensive treatment, for its portrayal of the journey of the psychic self to a state of realization, in a world characterized by evil and complacency. As the story begins, Edward and Mary Darnell share a good life: they are financially stable, they have established a mutually satisfying household routine, and they are in love. Yet Edward harbors a gentle, unfulfilled desire to demonstrate (physically) his tender passion for his beloved, whom he describes (to himself) as a woodland nymph. Mary shares her husband's feelings, but she is held back by a learned reticence, a cultural taboo against feminine passion. That their existence is placid and comfortable is evinced by the fact that their greatest concern is how to spend a one-hundred-pound windfall, a dilemma that leads to a protracted discussion of how to fit up their spare room with the money; the energy they spend in studying this problem diffuses their pent-up longing, and conversations about furniture stand in for words of love.

Thankfully, Edward indulges from time to time in a fantasy that there is a faun—a free, wild thing—that lives inside him, thereby avoiding becoming the historical equivalent of *The Man in the Gray Flannel Suit* and preventing the atrophying of his imagination and soul. While looking over the spare room, considering how best to furnish it, he lights upon a cache of old family documents and portraits that remind him that he is descended from minor nobility and that he may someday be in line for an inheritance. These considerations ignite his simmering imagination, taking him back to his childhood, and a long-suppressed memory surfaces: a visit with his father to a remote farmhouse in Wales, where they heard the shriek of a woman in the attic and strange singing that "might be compared [. . .] to a certain chant indeed that summons the angels and archangels to assist in the great Sacrifice." The weird details of the visit are never fully explained, leaving readers to horrify themselves by their own conjectures as to the cause of the scream of the unseen woman, and Darnell's dark imaginings grow into an ecstasy that transcends his daily human experience as a clerk. This attitude of wonder is key to the transcendent experience in Machen. Rational explanations are counter-productive to this end.

When Mary asks Edward why he is so absorbed in the papers he found in the spare room, he tells her of his quest to discover Mystery, a quest he began long before they met. He was living in London then. Enthralled, she eagerly attends to her husband's strange confession. Edward is gratified that she does not dismiss his fantasy as child's play or mental aberration, and he is deeply moved by her unaffected interest as he reveals a part of himself that he has hitherto not dared to express. When Mary joins him on his transcendent journey to open himself to Mystery, he expresses the effulgence of the love he feels for her in the language of mysticism: "her eyes were as the wells in the wood of which Darnell dreamed in the night-time and in the day."

To find Mystery, he tells her, he mixed up his routine. He rose at three o'clock in the morning, to see the world in literally a different light. He (consciously) looked at everything anew (i.e., practiced purposeful looking), even when observing the commonplace things he saw every day, "as if I had on the magic spectacles in a fairy tale." He no longer walked past flowers simply because "there is scarcely a street . . . where you won't see one or other of such things as these"; instead, he took the time to notice them and to register their presence. He found that his experience of life was altogether different: "all the strange tales I had ever heard were in my head that morning."

A crisis develops when Mary's aunt needs a home. Alice Nixon has accused her husband of philandering, abusing, and plotting against her and asks for, and is given, permission to move in with the Darnell's. As the couple wrestles with the inconvenience of the scheme, each receives a special kind of joy from self-denial and active love. Soon after Alice's visit,

Mr. Nixon arrives and accuses his wife of belonging to a cult (the unorthodox, pagan-leaning church which she frequents) and of madness (madness and unorthodoxy are one and the same to him); he has her committed. The evidence is inconclusive as to whether Alice is delusional or sane, but clearly she is the more sympathetic character of the pair. Later, Edward and Mary come upon a mystical pamphlet, presumably dropped by Alice, suggesting the practice of cultish and Masonic-style secret rites and the worship of strange gods at her church; and they realize that such practices are generally regarded as proof of insanity by most people. Edward observes that "want of imagination is always equated with sanity"; therefore, because Aunt Alice is an unconventional and imaginative woman possessing eccentric habits and beliefs, her personal qualities must render her insane in the eyes of most people. For the Darnells, the psychic journey is rewarding; for Alice, the journey toward self-awakening ends in incarceration in Bedlam.

Darnell's shamanistic, inward journey builds toward a sensual, sexual, and spiritual epiphany. When his wife joins him on his quest, their mutual love—newly released from the inhibitions that characterize their relationship at the beginning of the story—builds to a tension so great that a spiritual and emotional climax is inevitable: "there seemed to be gathering on all sides grotesque and fantastic shapes, omens of confusion and disorder, threats of madness, a strange company from another world."

The journey of the Darnell's commences with Edward's seeing the "wells" in Mary's eyes; and the imagery of the well reverberates throughout the work, unto the end, when the Darnell's achieve a transformation which is transcendent, a life fully experienced:

> So I awoke from a dream of a London suburb, of daily labour, of weary, useless little things; and as my eyes were opened I saw that I was in an ancient wood, where a clear well rose into grey film and vapour beneath a misty, glimmering heat. And a form came towards me from the hidden places of the wood, and my love and I were united by the well.

In the works of Machen, the psychic journey is a profoundly sensual expression of self, far far removed from the clinical and intellectual pretensions of psychiatry that he mocks in "Scrooge and the Spirit of Psycho-Analysis."

From the early "The Great God Pan" to the acidic satires he wrote later in life, Machen explored the roles of wonder and evil in human existence. He was at the height of his craft when he indited "The White People," *The Hill of Dreams,* and "A Fragment of Life," and the spellbinding prose of this period combines the seductive poetry of the Song of Songs, the archaic chivalry of the Arthurian Grail mythology, the magic of the fairy tale, and a Whitmanesque spiritual awakening. Yet in Machen beauty and love are entwined with insanity and horror.

A New Lovecraftian Writer in Our Midst

Michael D. Miller

TONY LaMALFA. *Forbidden Knowledge: Two Tales of Lovecraftian Terror*. New York: Hippocampus Press, 2023. 147 pp. $10.00 tpb. ISBN: 9781614984122.

And the critics have said . . .

> The pair of novellas in *Forbidden Knowledge* constitute some of the most vibrant and chilling ventures into Lovecraftian fiction in recent decades. Tony LaMalfa has captured the atmosphere of Lovecraft's work—whether it be the cloistered halls of Miskatonic University in "The Face on the Floor" of the hints of aquatic Deep Ones in "If Only Skin Deep"—with a skill and elegance that renders each tale a richly textured excursion into cosmic horror.—S. T. JOSHI

> With *Forbidden Knowledge*, Tony LaMalfa has created a pair of novellas so well-versed in the oeuvre of Lovecraft, he had me convinced—at times—I was reading an undiscovered work by Lovecraft himself. But *Forbidden Knowledge* is far too dynamic, unsettling, and utterly original to be anything other than the work of an explosive new talent, a talent whose prose burns like a white-hot star from beyond the fourth dimension.—CHRISTA CARMEN

So is *Forbidden Knowledge* and author Tony LaMalfa truly as meritorious as inscribed by these accolades?

What exactly is "Lovecraftian" fiction? On one tentacle we have the classic pastiche type story that will reference a book, alien entity, character, setting, or object from a Lovecraft story. On another it is simply (or densely) using Lovecraft's cosmic viewpoint as the horror/monster of the narrative. It has been argued for years whether the simple borrowing of Lovecraft place names for instance is more of an attempt to write another "Cthulhu Mythos" story than to explore the implications of cosmicism on human existence. Lin Carter suggested as far back as his 1972 book *Lovecraft: A Look Behind the Cthulhu Mythos* that a certain number of these would be required to be even remotely "Lovecraftian." Those types of stories would have a Mythos book (*The Necronomicon*), setting (Miskatonic University), and entity (Yog-Sothoth), and some writers may even "contribute" their versions of these Lovecraftian tropes (adding books, places, and entities to the unending catalogue of Lovecraftian inventory). Carter did specify that the allure of such pastiches was actually in filling the gaps existing in the Mythos with new stories to add to the canon. Modern Lovecraftian fiction has evolved beyond that, focusing on the cosmic horror element in worlds and experiences unique to each author. Yet there still exist unending classic pastiche stories where one can't get enough of a Deep One or another volume of forbidden lore. I will point out from the beginning that LaMalfa's two novellas are all and none of that.

One of the elements of the truly Lovecraftian is the style of the prose, which should be phrased with such skill as to invoke the proper mood and atmosphere. Not only does LaMalfa's style recall Lovecraft at his most restrained, but it also bears even more striking similarity to Poe, arguably the greatest influence on Lovecraft. The first novella, "The Face on the Floor," even alludes to Poe by the second page. Here are a few glimpses of LaMalfa's vibrant descriptions:

> Just then a distant piping, more melodic than menacing, became audible somewhere beyond consciousness. With eyes fixed on nothing in particular, my vision began to blur, and the regal patterns of lacy fabric blended together to form a towering blanket of snow that rose incredibly high in every direction! At first, I marveled at its sheer vastness and ivory beauty; but as the snow solidified into an icy wall, so did my fear of becoming infinitesimal in comparison . . .

> These ruminations gave way to a torrent of dark imaginings and damnable analogies inspired by memory loss of this

one individual, yet easily applicable to the entire human race's insular survival in blissful ignorance of the planet's true esoteric and primordial history. Had our species fallen victim to the cruel trick of some alien entity unseen by the waking eye?

[. . .] If one survives the rending of one's very consciousness to glimpse such demoniac locales—most likely in a dream state—one may begin to comprehend both the splendor and the cost of these esoteric offerings, which are gifts of the fifth dimension and borrowed briefly, only to be returned to the giver unwrapped yet never fully understood . . .

LaMalfa's novellas are filled with passages like these, the entire prose an enjoyment to read and contributing deliberately to the skillful effect of these stories.

Rather than filling gaps in the Lovecraft Mythos, LaMalfa does the opposite by expanding these openings and delivering better results as Lovecraftian fiction. "The Face on the Floor," set in 1927, takes the character of Jonathan Charles Danforth from *At the Mountains of Madness*, of whom we are only given a simple detail of a debilitating past experience reading the *Necronomicon*. LaMalfa tells us the story of that event. As a student at Miskatonic University skilled in Latin, he is hired by one Andre Oswald to access the Latin copy (translated by Olaus Wormius and printed in Spain during the seventeenth century) of that abhorred tome and translate a few specific passages. Along the way we encounter a number of Lovecraft characters, Nathaniel Wingate Peaslee, Dr. Armitage (during the events of "The Dunwich Horror"), Albert Wilmarth, and other curiosities such as the Nathaniel Pickman Derby Foundation, the *Arkham Advertiser*, and references to classicism à la "the forge of Hephaestus." LaMalfa is well versed in the Mythos traditions. The narrative of the story ends with Danforth's invitation to join Professor Dyer's upcoming expedition to Antarctica. Thus, this story serves not only as a precursor to *At the Mountains of Madness*, but invites us to revisit that work, knowing what we now know about Danforth and why he was driven to insanity in Lovecraft's original masterpiece.

The second novella, "If Only Skin Deep," is looser with the

Lovecraftian references, and more solidly an original work, less concerned with expanding the existing Mythos but more with spreading the Mythos to new undiscovered areas. This story, taking place in 1938, features another college student, Myriam Delacroix, and her adventure to conduct fieldwork studies on the Māori in New Zealand. Our Lovecraftian connections are simply that she is a friend of Lillian Danforth, sister of Jonathan (which as a plot device connects these two novellas), and that she is telling us the story as a confession in an asylum under the care of a "Dr. Danforth." The other Lovecraftian concept is importing and adding the worship of Dagon and the heritage of the Deep Ones to the Māori. In a story similar to "The Shadow over Innsmouth," Myriam is essentially alone in her discoveries about the true ancestry of the Māori, but not alone in discovering that ancestry is a shared one—with her! The value of the story, like many of Lovecraft's, is to serve also as an education, and LaMalfa gives us several graduate cultural study courses on the Māori intermixed with the narrative.

The real success of these novellas is that LaMalfa makes us sympathetic to the protagonists in a way Lovecraft never could. Although it was never Lovecraft's intention to do so, modern Lovecraftian writing has always suffered by attempts to make the characters relatable to us to evoke more empathy. Typically, faulty choices often verge on tying characters to social or political demographics often irrelevant to the story. LaMalfa does not employ such trappings to ensnare our heartstrings; he simply lets the theme of "forbidden knowledge" do the work. Whether it is Danforth obsessing over the *Necronomicon*, losing all his friends, including a budding romance with Miss Shepley, a Miskatonic librarian, or Myriam blindly joining the cult of Dagon while cutting herself off from her only living relatives, we feel that loss as we are pulled into each of these protagonists' corruption and hope they can reverse course and save themselves. Quite the opposite to what we would typically expect for the fate of characters in a Lovecraftian scenario.

While the theme of forbidden knowledge is a classic Lovecraftian formula, it is the cosmic element that encapsulates the best Lovecraftian writing, and LaMalfa is not deficient in that ultimate revelation.

> It seemed impractical to disembark the vestigial vessel upon which I was now sailing across treacherous seas of transcendental secrets. And wandering aimlessly through the wonts of everyday life, filled with routine and predictability, could never compare with my adventures into the unknown. It would be futile to look back at who I was after unmasking the face of God, or rather, the epicenter of the universe with its boundless borders of expansion and contraction . . .

Forbidden Knowledge is everything the critics say it is and more. These first novellas seem to have come out of nowhere and may have been a risk for publication, but they are a win. The long story behind it is that LaMalfa—with no literary background—sent the draft of "The Face on the Floor" in 2019 to S. T. Joshi, who recognized its potential immediately. However, it was a long two-year struggle to find publication, two years where LaMalfa honed his skills and produced "If Only Skin Deep." In 2022 the idea for a double-feature debut was conceived, and Hippocampus Press carried out the birthing. *Forbidden Knowledge* is in the cosmic house! If the stars are right, I foresee this work will be well rewarded and additional genuine Lovecraftian yarns from LaMalfa will follow.

Half Sunk a Shattered Visage Lies

Daniel Pietersen

HENRY BARTHOLOMEW, ed. *The Living Stone: Stories of Uncanny Sculpture, 1858–1943*. N.p.: Handheld Press, 2023. 244 pp. $18.99 tpb. ISBN: 9781912766765.

I was terrified by lots of things as a child. Some of them justifiably, many of them not. One of the more memorable things, and you can decide for yourself whether this is justifiable or not, was the 1963 film *Jason and the Argonauts*, directed by Don Chaffey and with special effects by the legendary Ray Harryhausen. A favorite of Easter bank holiday TV scheduling, it was never the fickle gods or fearsome monsters that scared me. I wasn't even that frightened of the infamous skeletal warriors—who burst from the ground in the film's finale and are instructed by their master, the sorcerous Aeëtes, to "Kill! Kill! Kill them all!"—because skeletal warriors are, frankly, pretty cool. No, what terrified me as a child and still unnerves me as an adult was a single shot from much earlier in the film. More accurately, what terrified me was a single sound.

While exploring the Isle of Bronze for provisions, the Argonauts Hercules and Hylas make the unwise decision to steal from an apparently unguarded treasure chamber hidden in the pedestal of an immense statue of a figure named Talos. As they leave they are disturbed by strange noises, reminiscent of flowing water and hissing steam. The camera angle suddenly cuts to a view that looks over the shoulder of Hercules and up to the huge statue as it gazes out to sea. Hercules, for all his strength and courage, looks very small indeed. Suddenly, with a tortured screech of metal the statue's head turns to glare directly at the heroic demigod and, by doing so, glares directly at us, the less heroic viewer. In just a few seconds Talos is transformed from an impressive yet inert piece of statuary and into an animate, dangerous creature.

It is a scene that plays with, and then snaps, our understanding of how the animate and inanimate are fundamentally different. It seems somehow more comprehensible that even the once-living, like Aeëtes' skeletons, could be made to move again than the never-living should rise and turn against us.

This fracture between the animate and the inanimate, and how one can become the other, is the core focus of *The Living Stone*, Handheld Press's latest anthology of weird and unsettling short fiction. Editor Henry Bartholomew explores this flux of being by talking about the strange qualities of a statue's being: "Our sensory experience of [a statue], especially of large statuary, is never total. It cannot be experienced from a single viewpoint but retains haptic depths and surfaces that reveal themselves as the viewer changes their position." In other words, the statue we see or touch through our senses is only part of our full experience of the statue; we rely on our memory or imagination to fill in those parts our senses cannot reach. As much as statues are undeniably solid, material things-in-the-world, creations that often far outlast their creator, they are also as nebulous and indistinct as our fallible minds can make them. Shadows play across their carved faces, drawing leers and grimaces from immobile stone. They quickly become deeply uncanny; somehow far worse in their frozen stasis than Freud's ur-example of a human corpse.

This uncanniness is at the heart of Bernard Capes's brief "The Marble Hands," where a sculpture of a dead woman's hands sits in place of a headstone over her grave. Capes uses this eerie image to investigate not just how representations of human beings can be strange but how human body parts, hands especially, can become strange—"wicked and unclean," the narrator admits—when separated from the bodily whole. It is a deeply affecting tale for all its brevity, and the long-held childhood terror of its now-adult narrator as hard, sun-warmed stone turns "soft and cold, like dead meat" is quite palpable. This malevolence of stone is repeated in "The Statue," by James Causey, as a meek and penniless sculptor's creation becomes a post-mortem vessel for all his hatred and vengeance. This is a sinister and suspenseful tale as life comes to the eponymous statue in a suitably half-seen, zoetropic fashion but also a cautionary one for those who care more for an artwork's value than they do for its worth. The statue being that of a child also doubles its uncanniness and makes the reader think again of that clash between immediate appearances and the hidden world of statues. The malevolence continues more openly in Clark Ashton Smith's "The Maker of Gargoyles," devolving eventually into open mayhem. A less fantastically weird offering than some of Smith's work, the realism of his Averoigne setting serves to make the nocturnal assault of two terrifying gargoyles on the city of Vyones all the more claustrophobic.

The high-point of the anthology is, however, undoubtedly "Benlian," by the Yorkshire-born writer Oliver Onions. Perhaps best known for the oft-collected tale "The Beckoning Fair One," Onions's "Benlian" is his masterwork, in my opinion; a deeply unsettling vision of obsession and delusion that develops as the narrator, known only as "Pudgie," slowly unravels from a position of cynicism and skepticism and ultimately becomes the thrall of the cadaverous sculptor Benlian, as the latter attempts to "pass into" the form of a strange malformed yet godlike statue. How much of the story is due to Pudgie's feverish mental state—which Onions sketches in beautifully through increasingly breathless and agog narration—is left up to the reader, and it's a testament to Onions's skill and confidence that he is happy to leave the tale hanging ambivalently. This skill is, in fact, so deftly employed that Lovecraft's "Hypnos"—a similar tale of thralldom and the transition of flesh into stone that appears later in the anthology—feels derivative in comparison.

A couple of the tales did drag slightly for me. Edith Wharton's "The Duchess at Prayer" is florid and atmospheric but suffers from a rendition of archaically courtly dialogue that rapidly grates, while "A Marble Woman," by W. C. Morrow, makes overmuch of a fairly well-telegraphed twist. These are balanced out, however, by the languid, decadent horror of Robert W. Chambers's "The Mask," part of his wider cycle of *The King in Yellow*, or "The Living Stone" itself. Written by E. R. Punshon, the tale that gives its name to the anthology is weirdly reminiscent of Nigel Kneale and his ideas that antiquity can itself become a form of life, or at least a desire for life. Punshon, without really fully describing the situation, manages to make inert rock become vile and predatory; a crouching thing that draws the unwitting and then, without mouth or teeth, devours them. It makes me think of the weirdness and confusion at the heart of *Picnic at Hanging Rock*, that other classic of the lithic made strange.

Another immensely successful publication from Handheld, with an erudite and fascinating introduction from Bartholomew. Not for every reader of horror fiction, certainly, but a delight for those of us who need to check, with a nervous glance, if the gargoyle illustrating the cover hasn't perhaps moved just ever so slightly.

Covid Horrors

S. T. Joshi

RAMSEY CAMPBELL. *The Lonely Lands.* London & New York: Flame Tree Press, 2023. 246 pp. $26.95 (£20) hc. ISBN: 9781787588655; $16.95 (£9.95) tpb. ISBN: 9781787588622.

No one can say that Ramsey Campbell, at the venerable age of seventy-seven, isn't up-to-date. In this new novel he takes on one of the most traumatic and divisive events of our time—the Covid pandemic—and uses it as the springboard for a gripping and literally nightmarish novel that tiptoes between supernatural and psychological horror at every turn.

The Lonely Lands is largely focused on Joe Hunter, a man in the Liverpool area who, after his partner Dawn leaves him for another man, finds love and companionship with Olivia, who runs an antique shop with the distinctive (and significant) name Made of Memories. But Joe admits to Olivia that his childhood was not an entirely tranquil one, largely because he lived in actual terror of his grandfather, Arthur Maine. Maine had been a follower of a church run by the charismatic Christian Noble. Readers of Campbell's work will recognise that name from his recent Daoloth trilogy, where Noble is presented as one who believes in the literal resurrection of the dead—and apparently has perfected a means of bringing that about.

Indeed, Arthur speaks in ominous tones that the living can effect such a resurrection merely by thinking about the dead, or dreaming about them. On his deathbed he urges his grandson, "Just promise me you'll think good thoughts about me when you haven't got me any more." This adjuration is far more than the conventional *De mortuis nil nisi bonum.* Arthur goes on to say of the people in Noble's congregation: "Mr Noble used to help them see their loved ones . . . only half the time they hardly recognised them. They couldn't keep their shape, the one they used to have or the one they'd turned into either." And, finally,

"I heard him say once all of us are just cocoons for the dead."

Joe, distressingly, finds himself in a position to test Noble's theories. A burglar who had broken into a neighbouring shop had coughed on Olivia as she tried to detain him. Joe, for his part, had seen the entire incident, but couldn't reach Olivia because a mob of aggressive anti-Covid protesters had barred his way. Although the burglar, Darrell Swann, is arrested (and later given a nominal jail sentence), Joe watches helplessly as his wife succumbs to Covid and dies.

What follows, throughout the rest of the novel, is an utterly disorienting series of tableaux where the reader doesn't know whether the event is occurring or is a dream on Joe's part or a hallucination whereby his memories have become twisted—perhaps through the influence of the dead. There are repeated scenes of Joe searching for Olivia while vacationing in Greece. He finds her and leads her back to their hotel—but the oddness of their conversation means that something has gone horribly wrong with Joe's memories, or else that Olivia has in some fashion returned from the dead ("Their embrace felt disconcertingly insubstantial").

Some of these dreams or hallucinations come across as grotesquely comical, as when Joe imagines he has donned utterly inappropriate attire for his wedding day; but even in the dream he knows something is awry ("It wasn't like this . . . This didn't happen"). But another dream, where Olivia gives birth, not to a human baby, but to dozens or hundreds of hideous winged creatures ("naked midget simulacra"), is a moment of agonising horror. At other times Joe believes he is being pursued by the ghost or spirit or revenant of his grandfather. What might seem like a ludicrous chase through a car park (what we Americans call a parking garage) is in fact acutely terrifying as only Campbell can make it:

> He could only dash across the car park, though his flight felt like thoughtless panic. He didn't know whether he meant to flee into the street in search of somewhere else to lose the pursuit or retreat down the stairs again, though the prospect of returning to the lower regions felt like prolonging a nightmare. It was starting to seem possible that the chase would never end—that he was trapped in his personal eternity. He needed some-

thing to stop his grandfather, and he would have prayed if he'd thought it would be any use. "Please stop it" was the best he could manage, in a voice so muted it expected no response.

And yet, there is much more going on in *The Lonely Lands* than these isolated moments of dread. It is true that the overall tone of the work recalls his other masterworks that tread the borderline between dream and reality, such as *Incarnate* (1981) and *Needing Ghosts* (1990); but, as the tragic and infuriating manner of Olivia's death attests, Campbell also addresses some of the central social concerns in our post-pandemic age. How can one ensure public safety without infringing on individual freedom? Why is it that so many people rebel at authority even when it is not in their own self-interest to do so? Why is the criminal justice system so heavily weighted toward protecting a defendant but not on rendering justice for the victim? These are not issues that writers of horror fiction customarily discuss, but Campbell has developed a mastery in incorporating them seamlessly into his weird narratives. Indeed, it could well be said that Ramsey Campbell—like some of the mainstream writers upon whose work he nurtured himself in earlier days, ranging from Graham Greene to Vladimir Nabokov—has long been one of the leading social satirists of our age, a kind of modern-day Martin Amis or even Ambrose Bierce. And it should not be assumed that his satire is solely directed toward conservative or working-class people: in a pungent scene he laces into an overprotective parent who mouths conventional liberal platitudes in steering her son away from books that might cause him to question the worldview she has carefully inculcated in him.

But we will remember *The Lonely Lands* for its many scenes of unnerving terror. Even if many of the chapters come across as more or less independent scenes with no intimate relation to one another, the cumulative effect of the novel is the inducement of a profound unease in the reader in regard to the nebulous distinction between dream, memory, and reality. And the conclusion, where Joe commits an utterly selfless act to preserve his wife's memory in the afterlife, allows the novel to end on a note of mingled poignancy and horror.

The Lonely Lands may lack the flamboyant, over-the-top

gruesomeness that many contemporary readers lamentably have come to expect, but the more pervasive sense of the uncanny that it effortlessly engenders places it high among Campbell's output—and that means it holds a very high place indeed in the weird fiction of our time.

Hungry

Taylor Trabulus

"That was the day I killed my mom," Jackie said, shaking her head as if that would make it all come untrue. The reporter across the table handed her a tissue as tears ricocheted down her quivering chin. Jackie was being interviewed about her experience on February 2nd, the day when the side effects from the diet drug Triazepan started to surface in her mother. It was now March 3rd, thirty days from that day she now sat at the table with the reporter.

When Triazepan went onto the market it quickly became a necessity for anyone in Hollywood, the fashion industry, and whoever else could get their hands on it and wanted to lose weight, or keep weight off, with relative ease. It worked so simply by suppressing an appetite for food and stopping any feelings of hunger. Of course, there were more minor, more immediate side effects from taking the drug, such as nausea and vomiting, diarrhea, constipation, dizziness, skin rash, hair loss, dry mouth, hallucinations, insomnia, mood swings, loss of hearing, loss of sight, and kidney failure. But the guaranteed results far outweighed any of *those* trivialities. And, as if overnight, celebrities and doctors alike were singing its praises all over social media, in magazines, and on talk shows and podcasts.

The first incident happened when an actress on a movie set in Montana bit a chunk out of her co-star's cheek, quickly gobbling it down before lunging at him for more. Despite the crew's efforts to restrain her, the actress escaped from the set. It took more than an hour for the police to find her in a nearby barn munching on the foot of an elderly farmer, the tiny bones of his toes crunching under the weight of her clamorous teeth. It was reported that she charged the officers and they had no choice but to shoot her five times until she finally stopped attacking them.

The authorities said that something in her had just snapped. But when similar behavior occurred with a male model at a fitting in New York and then a woman in a Pilates class in Los Angeles, it was clear that a pattern was emerging. In each case their eyes turned to black, they started to drool incessantly, and they became ravenously hungry for human flesh. It took weeks for anyone to make the final connection that they had all been prescribed Triazepan only a month before these incidents. A month before February 2nd was around the time Jackie's mom had come home from the doctor with her first dose.

"She got it to take off ten pounds before my cousin's bar mitzvah," Jackie explained. "It only took a couple of weeks for her to fit into this dress she had been dying to buy. We thought it was a miracle drug—she was *so* skinny. "

"Aw, that's sweet," the reporter said, pretending to care but eager to move on to the real reason she had asked Jackie to the café. "Let's talk about the day when she started to react to the medication."

Jackie nodded and took a deep breath in. "Well, it was like any other Wednesday. We got into the car, and we always went to my little brother's school to drop him off first. When we got there, Mom parked and walked him into class. I waited in the front seat and called my friend Becca to ask her about a test we had that day . . . then I heard the most horrible screams.

"When I looked out the window, I saw people running away from the school, so I hung up on Becca and rushed over to the scene where the others were running from. And then I saw . . ."

Jackie paused and made an effort to sip her tea with a trembling hand, but instead spilled most of it onto the table. She let out her breath, as if she had been holding it in this whole time, and dabbed at the spill with her napkin.

"What did you see?" The reporter nudged her along.

"I saw a woman eating a boy. She was tearing the flesh off his back, piece by piece, with her long-manicured nails and nibbling on it. Tiny morsels of meat kept flying out of her mouth while she chewed. Bloody drool was dripping down her face and she kept licking it up like it was chocolate sauce. Then I heard something in the bushes. It was my brother, so I started sprinting over to him, but someone rushed at me and bit my arm."

Jackie rubbed her arm where she was bitten, now a nasty scar, a battle wound, and promptly continued:

"I pushed the person off me, and they fell to the ground. That's when I realized it was my mom. So, I screamed at her. I yelled at her about what was happening and why she bit me. She wouldn't answer me. She was like a wild animal, snarling at me on all fours. And then she looked over to the bushes where my brother was. It was like she was smelling the air—like she could smell him, like she was sniffing out some sort of prey . . . she was quickly crawling toward him.

"I didn't even think, I just picked up the shovel next to me on the grass and hit her over the head. I didn't mean to kill her! That was just all it took to break her neck! Or . . . I think that's what happened. It looked like a bone was jutting out of the side of her throat, but she didn't even seem to notice what had happened. I grabbed my brother. When we left her, she still had this hunger in her eyes and she was flicking her tongue in the air, trying to catch any drops of blood rolling off her mangled body. It was like she was possessed!"

Jackie now spoke hastily and in a raised voice, drawing attention from the other customers in the café. The reporter looked around, nodding to reassure them everything was all right.

"I just wish we knew sooner. How could they let a drug like that go on the market? All those people who . . ." Jackie started to tear up again. "And you know what happened to them all."

Jackie was referring to all the others who had taken Triazepan. It all depended on the time when they took their first dose. Usually, the incubation period was 30 days, but sometimes the effects occurred sooner. No one had shown immunity, and no one had yet survived the . . . reaction. Anyone who took it had changed, had attacked, and had been shot by police or killed by worried Samaritans trying to defend themselves or others. Triazepan had been swiftly removed from public access once the connection had been made clear. Incidents were becoming fewer and fewer, but there were still cases that popped up and needed to be dealt with.

"And they still can't figure out exactly why it happened. I don't think we'll ever have answers. It's all so horrifying!" Jackie howled, sobbing through her words and aggressively picking at the scar on her arm which was growing more inflamed as she became increasingly upset.

The reporter patted Jackie's hand to console her. She crouched down to her purse to get Jackie another tissue. When she looked back up again, Jackie's eyes were black, and she was drooling.

Cultists Descend upon Portland: The H. P. Lovecraft Film Festival

Katherine Kerestman

Breaking News: Hordes of black-cloaked-and-hooded-cultists filled the streets of Portland, Oregon, over the weekend. They swarmed into area restaurants—particularly Sam's Billiards, where they were rumored to be sucking Bloody Marys and Bloody Howards from dawn until well past the witching hour. From there, they passed drunkenly into the antient streets, invading hostelries and shops. They reassembled, it is said, at the Hollywood Theater, a century-old landmark, where they performed unhallowed rites. Although I followed them in the role of investigator, I fell under their psychic control. I—who cannot carry a tune—became the Anthropomorphic Tabernacle Choir Leader at the Cthulhu Prayer Breakfast of the Esoteric Order of Dagon, an annual event for many years running.

How I came to be leading the acolyte choir of gibber and jabber, which belted out—to the tunes of "We Will Raise Him Up," "I Am the Bread of Life," "Kumbaya," "Bound for the Promised Land," and "Salve Regina"—hideous hymns from infernal regions, I shall never know. The choir followed not these melodies, and thus I was compelled to order them to sing howsoever they chose. The result was a horrific chorus of blasphemous cacophony, after which the Hierophant led the congregation in Darrell Schweitzer's "Let's Gibber Now of Yog-Sothoth":

> Iä! Iä! Iä! Let the Earth abhor thee!
> It won't do mankind that much good
> When old ones are set free!
> we offer up our virgins,
> when the stars are just right.
> Give us a monstrous birth, to open up the gate!

John Skipp, Sergeant of Optimism, prophesied to the ghoulish congregation: "The oceans will not turn black and the sky will not descend upon us . . . we'll be bobbing for apples—*great apples with teeth!*"

Tony LaMalfa, Lovecraftian writer and novitiate into the cult, leapt upon the altar, where the spirits moved him to cry out a dreadful testimonial of his honeymoon journey into the darkness of unnamable shades and weird sounds from the abyss. The hapless couple, being Tony and his bride, wallowing in marital bliss, found themselves stranded in a decrepit old house owned by a sinister couple who kept a wolf in their home. The needle of their gas tank was on Empty, strange sounds emanated from the void around the dwelling, and every DANGER indicator found in nature and catalogued in B-movies was manifested. By the time Brother LaMalfa had concluded his witness of the diabolical marital tour, the congregation was shuddering. I was moved to proffer my own testimony of a personal descent into dark realms:

On the day in question, a friend and I had been exploring the alleys and graveyards of Salem (I am fond of passing Halloween there). At midnight, there remained one final destination on our weird agenda: a visit to the headquarters of the Satanic Temple. According to its website, the Satanic Temple espouses a mission of, not Satan-worship, but anti-religion. Satanic Templars assert their right to show their statue of Baphomet in public spaces, as various religions display their own symbols. The Satanic Temple is housed in an old funeral home building, which looks like a fraternity house. We could hear people plodding heavily on the vocal floorboards of the second floor of the two-story frame structure.

We began our exploration in the Ouija Board Room, a large chamber upon the walls of which hangs a collection of historic Ouija boards. Then we ventured into the galleries that house Satanic art, primarily statuary and paint-on-canvas renderings of the Satanic Kiss, which works were generally well executed. We browsed the collection of historical documents that included newspaper articles of the 1980s and 1990s, reflecting the Satanic Cult Paranoia of that period. At that time, you may recall, parents labeled and banned—even burned—

records that, when played backwards, unleashed unholy incantations upon tender and innocent ears. We asked about the Baphomet Statue, and we were told that we had to wait, because another couple was viewing it. It was in the back yard, we were told. Only one person or couple could go back there at a time, they said.

To recap: It was midnight. We had been interacting with witches (alive and historical Dead witches) all day. We were in the headquarters of the Satanic Temple, formerly a funeral home, with foot-clomping going on over our heads. We were to be separated from other people. In the dark. Behind the house. After midnight. To see the Baphomet Statue.

Every praeternatural alarum deployed in my body. In plain terms, I freaked out! All my physical and emotional reflexes screamed, "Get out! NOW! Don't go there—alone—in the dark—after midnight! Are you crazy?"

I grabbed my friend by the arm, urged, "Let's get out of here." He did not understand. I was forced to spell it out. Maybe they are worshipping Satan, I whispered, desperately trying not to draw attention to myself. Maybe we were intended as a Sacrifice. I had watched too many Hammer films to not know when it was not safe to Go There—separated from other people—in the dark—behind the Satanic Temple headquarters—an old funeral home—on the outskirts of Salem, Massachusetts—after midnight.

This is the first time I have put down this experience in writing. Six or eight years have passed. I do not know if I am still being watched. I know too much.

The Hierophant seized the microphone from my sweating palm. Gravely he intoned the benediction: "May nothing happen to you until you are no longer useful," whereupon the congregation dispersed into the narrow streets of the old city. Iä! Iä! Cthulhu fhtagn!

The cultists emerged in other terrifying outcroppings. The Hollywood Theater became a morass of ebony-cloaked figures and other entities sprouting tentacles, claws, and wings. Together they viewed numerous short and hideous films and some loathsome feature-length movies, shown in the three shadowy dungeons of the Hollywood. Some attended panels on such topics as "H. P. Lovecraft and Cats," "Putting Cosmic Horror on the Screen," and "Manifesting Mythos: Cosmic Terror in the Ancient." Others swelled the rooms of the library across the street, listening to author dronings, from which multitudes of terrified patrons fled into the street. The greatest concentration of acolytes was about the Patriarch of the Weird, S. T. Joshi, whose legions of idolatrous followers jostled to pay homage to the High Priest, the representative of Howard on earth. By their looks, a number of cultists gave me fair warning that I would henceforth be watched. While I was thankful that I never carry a cellphone surveillance device, still I wonder if, somehow, they had managed to implant an obscene device or spore in my body.

I did my utmost to put them off my trail. Trying to shake them, I took two tours to the edges of this no-man's land: one to Cannon Beach (in a dangerous storm, the variety that causes ships to wreck on the rock-lined coastline, and which prevented me from disembarking from the van—had I been cursed?) and one to the Columbia River Gorge Waterfalls and Mt. Hood. The latter tour brought me to the Timberlake Lodge. At least, that is what They said. I just happen to be savvy enough that I know the Overlook Hotel when I see it—why, even on our approach I recognized the façade and even the window from which mother and child escape a possessed Johnny. I stomped inside the rustic mountain lodge and demanded that they hand over the evidence—Johnny's axe. I immediately verified that it *was* Johnny's axe—because, burned into the wooden handle, were the words "Here's Johnny!" They can't pull the wool over Creepy Cat's eyes!

Portland is all about occult cultists' rites and obscene cover-ups. Even their motto—reiterated on an untold number of bumper stickers—is "Keep Portland Weird." I can smell a conspiracy theory a mile away. The driver of the Oregon Coast tour admitted that the entire region is accursed. It is a *Six-Year Curse*, he said. Way back, in 1930, more than a million acres of primeval forest burned in a forest fire. Extensive logging had resulted in dragging the trees out of the forest and leaving a trail of dried wood debris on the forest floor. The kindling erupted in a conflagration of which the devil would be proud. Old-growth forests naturally contain little ground cover, and the trees in them are spaced widely apart; but forests that have been replanted after the clear-cutting of the original trees are characterized by tightly packed trees with an increased risk of fire. Every six years a major fire erupted in the Portland area. And that is how the inhabitants of the accursed land became aware that they were the victims of a hellish curse.

Our dauntless tour guide brought the unsuspecting tour group to Cannon Beach for shopping and for lunch. Lewis and Clark had camped here in 1805 and 1806, when, with the assistance of a female Indigenous guide, they were in quest of a Northwest Passage. When they reached the Pacific Ocean, they finally figured out that there was no direct water route from the Atlantic to the Pacific.

Shipwrecks have occurred up and down this rocky coast. The ocean roils here, earning it the moniker "Graveyard of the Pacific." Undetected, shoals move beneath the frothy waves and scalp the hulls of hapless vessels. Long ago, a Spanish galleon broke apart upon these rocks. Twenty years later, it is said, an iron cannon was heaved from the depths upon the shore in a location since named Cannon Beach. Neahkahnie Mountain tumbles and crashes into the surf here. Here, too, the survivors of the ill-fated Spanish galleon are rumored to have buried their booty—doubloons and jewels, a Prince of Darkness's ransom. Numerous elk graze on the grassy banks of the estuary, and Haystack Rock juts from the white-capped water like a Titan's fist thrust menacingly from the deep. Other jagged rocks protrude like the razor-sharp teeth in a sea-monster's maw. Tsunamis have not occurred in this region since the eighteenth century, but the movement of tectonic plates here indicates that earthquakes (and subsequent tsunamis) are bound to happen sometime. As our van cruised Highway 101 and OR 26, I became aware of all the logging trucks tailing us—great long logs on long vehicles. I'm sure that they were from Twin Peaks. And you know what that means.

Desperately hoping that I had, this time, evaded the cultist scouts, I decided to reconnoiter the curiosities of Portland. To this end, I took a Portland Spirit river cruise. Below deck, I questioned a weird passenger—a woman who spoke with a British accent! What was she doing here? She alleged that her mother had attended a high-end nanny school in Whitby (Whitby, England, where Dracula came ashore in the derelict *Demeter,* arriving in storm and fury to wreak havoc upon Christendom and proper Englishmen and Englishwomen). The English lady went on to say that her mother had been nanny to Mick Jagger. I laid a portion of the Blame at her feet. The English lady dared not deny it.

Oregon is a land of rugged and lethal coasts, roiling oceans, numerous volcanic mountains, eerie dark forests, psychotic demon-riddled axe-murderers who lurk in hotels closed for the winter and in hedge mazes, cougars, black bears, Cthulhu cultists, and shrouding mists that envelop the temperate rainforest coast and creep undetected into the cities, where they obscure the ancient secrets hid behind the veil.

Despite the persistent darkness of a gloomy sky and the threats of personal annihilation by cultists and axe-murderous authors, I made an astounding discovery: Oregon has no sales tax! Freed of that burden, I skulked the retail establishments (overcoming my apprehensions) and visited the Freakybuttrue Peculiarium and Powell's City of Books. Armed with my list of out-of-print titles, I went to the latter first. I was disappointed, though, for despite its immense size (the building takes up a city block and has several floors), I found not one thing on my list. The cashier said that many literary pilgrims are disappointed, for Powell's carries new books more than used ones. I purchased some volumes of Ligotti. As I chatted in the coffee shop with another customer, we noticed that it rained outside of one window, and then outside of another, but not outside of both windows at the same time. I blamed this diabolical phenomenon on the black cloud that follows me everywhere. The Freakybuttrue Peculiarium, on the other hand, exceeded my expectations! In this small but crazy monster museum, I found myself face-to-face with a Fishman from Lovecraft's Innsmouth, Bigfoot, a dune buggy monster, a pair of alien vivisectors, a doll's house from hell, and a vampire-slaying kit. The staff were very friendly, and even lighthearted.

The customers were as gleeful as schoolchildren playing hooky or zombies pulling out the intestines of their victims. I urge monster-loving people to visit this creepy establishment when in Portland.

At nightfall I returned to my hotel, for I had an early flight home.

I fell asleep making plans for next year's H. P. Lovecraft Film Festival, because I've been initiated into the cult.

An Interview with Ellen Datlow

Darrell Schweitzer

Conducted for the Philadelphia Science Fiction Society on Zoom, Friday, May 12, 2023.

Ellen Datlow needs no introduction, but to be brief: she was fiction editor of *Omni* magazine for seventeen years. She has edited more than a hundred anthologies and has been editing a *Best Horror of the Year* anthology (in different iterations) for thirty-six years. She acquires and edits short fiction and novellas for Tor.com. She has won scads of awards.

DS: Ellen, I admit I am in awe of the sheer number of anthologies you've done. I'd invite you at this point to hold up the latest one and plug it.

ED: I don't have one. I am finishing up reading for the *Best Horror* of 2022 (Volume Fifteen) and those are the books I have beside me here.

DS: What's the most recent one you've had published?

ED: [Pauses.] The most recent *original* one is *Screams from the Dark*—about monsters and the monstrous. Otherwise, there's *The Best Horror of the Year, Volume Fourteen* and *Body Shocks*, a reprint anthology of body horror, which just won a Splatterpunk Award.

DS: Miriam Siedel, who introduced us this evening, has actually done most of the homework. I know I have whole shelves of your anthologies. You've done more than a hundred. Myself have only done ten, the most recent of which is *Shadows out of Time* from PS Publishing. Obviously I am very small potatoes compared to you. I still wonder how you do it. You must spend all day, every day reading.

ED: [Laughs.] A lot of it, because I work on different projects at different times. I have several jobs. I acquire for Tor.com and I am always reading for a *Best of the Year* and am usually working on an original anthology, and sometimes another reprint anthology for Tachyon. So I can switch gears and take a break from reading horror and perhaps edit the science fiction or fantasy stories and novellas I've acquired for Tor.com. Also, I work from home. I get up from the computer and play with the cats. I get something to drink. Today I actually worked outside because the weather was beautiful. I grabbed a few anthologies I need to read for *The Year's Best* and just sat in the shade, which was nice. But I *am* reading a lot—that's my primary job (aside from editing).

DS: I suppose you have one advantage, which is sort of like being a World Fantasy Award judge. The only decision you have to make is whether this story is or is not good enough for *The Year's Best*. If it's not, you can stop and you don't have to write up any sort of report.

ED: Yes, but I sometimes get caught up in stories I know are not going to make it into *The Year's Best*. Unless a story is really bad, it's hard for me to just dismiss it and say, "Okay, I've seen that. I am not reading any more." If they're any good at all I get sucked in.

DS: So they might make your Honorable Mentions list.

ED: Yes. I also currently have two readers. I have one who lives in Washington State who reads electronic material that I'm pretty sure won't contain horror. I send her *Lightspeed*, On Spec, Aurealis, and a few other e-magazines and files. And I have a reader in New York to whom I pass on magazines and anthologies that I doubt will have anything I can use. I usually skim the October issue of *Asimov's* to make sure there is no horror in it because they've been running some dark material in that annual issue. But the rest of the run of *Asimov's* and all of *Analog* my reader reads, along with *Alfred Hitchcock's Mystery Magazine* and *Ellery Queen*. She reads them and lets me know when there's a story she thinks I should check out. Every year there seems to be an exponential increase in what I need to cover.

I was recently informed that only a few anthologies had been sent to the WFA judges this year. I've counted how many anthologies with horror that I received last year—there were around one hundred—and that's not counting the purely fantasy or the science fiction anthologies that *may* have some horror in them. There are hundreds. That means publishers are not sending the books to the judges, which is aggravating.

DS: You and I have both been judges, and what I've learned from experience is that the only way you can game the award is by sending the books in. Judges are heavily influenced by what they receive.

ED: That isn't "gaming" an award—it's just doing due diligence to get your work read. If a judge doesn't receive a work, they're not going to know it exists, unless it's a bestseller or has already made a splash in the field. The good thing about being a WFA judge is that you only have to do it once and you never will be asked again. What year did you do it, Darrell? I was a judge in 1987.

DS: I did it in 1991 for works published in 1990. So I am among the people who gave it to Neil Gaiman for a *Sandman* comic.

ED: And broke the system—some people got pissed off.

DS: Everyone seems to think that there is a rule against doing that again, but there isn't. We also had a tie between *Only Begotten Daughter* by James Morrow and *Thomas the Rhymer* by Ellen Kushner. So it was a good year. One of the advantages is you get a lot of nice books in the mail.

ED: However, after I judged I swore I would never read another Celtic fantasy. That was a year we received a *lot* of Celtic fantasies. Nope, no more.

DS: I've also looked over people's shoulders as they've been a judge. When George Scithers was a judge, he was farming some of the stuff out to his minions, so we were reading stuff and recommending things to him. I was actually very surprised by what they didn't receive.

But more to the point. I haven't always associated you with horror. Your earliest anthology that I can think of is *Alien Sex*, and then there was your editorship of *Omni*. So when did you start?

ED: When did I start getting into horror?

DS: Into editing.

ED: I worked in book publishing during the mid-'70s. I was in mainstream trade publishing, getting nowhere slowly, as I've often said. I worked for several publishers. Little, Brown was the first publishing job I had, in the New York office. I was sales secretary.

After that I went to Charterhouse (which was an imprint of David McKay) as an editorial assistant, and then I was moved to David McKay when the imprint was killed. I spent a miserable several months working for Donald I. Fine. Then I worked at Holt, Rinehart, and Winston for three years. My last job in book publishing was a short stint as assistant editor at Crown, working for the editor-in-chief, who was a bit unstable—I was fired.

At the time, *Omni* magazine was just starting out. Frank Kendig, who had published a non-fiction book for Holt, Rinehart, and Winston, was the first editor of *Omni*. And so Don Hutter, the executive editor [of Holt, Rinehart, and Winston] who had published Frank Kendig, and with whom I was still friendly, suggested I meet with Frank to talk about the possibility of some sort of job at *Omni*. I met with Frank, who introduced me to Fiction Editor Ben Bova. That whole summer, while I was unemployed I kept phoning and asking about work at the magazine. Ben did not have an assistant. He had a secretary who didn't read science fiction. This was 1979 and Ben was going to Brighton for the Worldcon. I was going to California for the first time. When I heard about Ben's trip I told him I could read the whole slushpile before he returned. I would be returning to New York a week before he was, and there was already a huge pile of unread manuscripts. He didn't know me from a hole in the wall, and initially said, "I don't think so," but he must have realized how much larger the pile would become while he was gone, so he called me back and said, "Yeah, sure, come and read the slush while I'm gone." I did catch up.

When Ben returned, he told me to hang around the office and ask the other editors if I could help them. The science editors. I'm sure they were saying to themselves, "Who the hell is this person who is volunteering to work for us?" I didn't know then that Ben was about to replace Frank Kendig as editor of the whole magazine. What I later learned was that this became a pattern of the magazine: every three years or so the editor was fired or quit, and a senior editor was promoted to that job—so there was a high turnover at the level of editor/ publisher.

Anyway, when Ben was promoted, they brought in Bob Sheckley as fiction editor. Bob Guccione and Kathy Keeton initially brought Ben on board to provide *Omni* with a kind of legitimacy, to counteract the reputation of *Omni's* sister magazine, *Penthouse*. Ben wanted to hire me with the title editorial assistant, but I insisted on a different title, because I'd already been working in publishing for several years. I asked for Associate Fiction Editor as a title and got it.

Bob Sheckley had no clue about working in an office. I don't know if he'd *ever* worked in an office before. He loved having an expense account. He smoked weed in the office. He offered me some and I said, "Nope. No thank you. I have to work."

Because neither of us knew how the process worked, I ended up reading everything. Usually the assistant reads slush and doesn't read the name writers—the fiction editor does. But neither Bob nor I knew the process, so I read all submissions first, except for the occasional friend of Bob's who sent him a story directly. So I gained a *lot* of experience. I remember having to phone Bob Silverberg. Before type was computerized, magazines were typeset manually, and so when an ad came in, you had to cut or add lines to stories—sometimes many lines! Anyway, it was the first time I'd ever spoken to Bob Silverberg, and I had to ask him to cut lines a few lines from his story. He said, "Who are you and why should I listen to you?" I just responded, "I'm Bob's assistant and this is what's going on." He finally warmed up and we did what we had to do.

Although I was reading science fiction when I got the job at *Omni*, I didn't know any of the writers personally. I was not in the field. I did not come from fandom. I came from mainstream book publishing. I loved science fiction and fantasy and horror, but I did not know the business of it.

DS: Why did you get into horror?

ED: At *Omni* we weren't supposed to publish horror, even though Ben had bought George R. R. Martin's "Sandkings." He considered it science fiction (it's actually sf/horror), so to him it was okay. We were not even supposed to buy fantasy. *Omni* started out to be strictly a science magazine with science fiction.

In any case, I was at *Omni* for about five years, when a *Penthouse* editor with whom I was friendly approached me and said, "I think I can get a book publication deal to produce several theme anthologies. Pitch me some ideas." So I pitched him three or four ideas. All would be wrapped around a handful of reprints that I'd wanted to but couldn't buy for *Omni*, the other half new stories solicited by me. Stories that were too sexual, or were horror stories, like "Down Among the Dead Men" by Gardner Dozois and Jack Dann and "The Monkey Treatment" by George R. R. Martin. I wanted both those stories for *Omni*, but Ben wouldn't let me. The first idea became *Blood Is Not Enough* and the other—about sex/gender relations—*Alien Sex*. The "deal" never came through, but a friend became my agent and sold both anthologies to book publishers.

I was deliberately avoiding a perceived conflict of interest of buying something for an anthology that I could have bought for *Omni*. After awhile I realized no one cared. The editors of *Omni* didn't care. After Ben Bova, few of them read the fiction. So that's how I got into editing horror, although I read it all along, from a young age.

DS: This was the editor at *Omni* who didn't read the fiction?

ED: Only one of the editors of the magazine after Ben read the fiction, unless I asked them to. An editor of a non-genre magazine can be the same as the editor-in-chief or publisher of the magazine. The first editor was Frank Kendig. Then Ben Bova, Richard Teresi, Gurney Williams, Patrice Adcroft, Keith Ferrell. Pamela Weintraub was the last one. The only one who cared about the fiction was Keith. After Ben, I was usually left alone to acquire what I chose (except for one editor in the middle).

When Dick Teresi took over from Ben and I had recently been made fiction editor (Sheckley left to go back to writing), "All My Darling Daughters" by Connie Willis was submitted. I loved the story, but felt uncomfortable about publishing it in *Omni*. I don't know how many of you have read it. It's pretty provocative. I asked Dick what he thought—I don't recall if he read it or not. I think not but I told him a little about the plot, and he basically said, "Do what you want." But I felt too anxious that early in my tenure to take a story that could have blown up things. Maybe it wouldn't have. I was more timid, when I was first promoted.

(Addendum: I've just realized that the story I told Dick about was "Her Furry Face" by Leigh Kennedy. It was just as provocative in its own way as the Willis. In any case, I turned down the Kennedy and the Willis, but reprinted both in *Alien Sex* when I had the chance.)

DS: I read that story when it was submitted to *Amazing*.

ED: What did you think?

DS: George Scithers wasn't having any. He felt that TSR would never have let him get away with it, and I think he was right.

ED: If they even read it . . .

DS: We actually had a galley of the final, unpublished volume of *New Dimensions*.

ED: Yes, it was in there. "Flying Saucer Rock and Roll" by Howard Waldrop that I published in *Omni* was from that ill-fated anthology. And "Dancing Chickens" by Ed Bryant. "Dancing Chickens." Mike Bishop eventually took "Dancing Chickens" for *Light Years and Dark*. We talked about it. I said, "It's a great story, but I can't buy it for *Omni*. You've got to take it." He had initially turned it down, but my pushing him changed his mind. The Bryant ended up in *Alien Sex* as well.

DS: There seem to be stories that everybody likes but nobody wants to publish. You probably know more about it than I do, but I've heard some of the editorial folklore about a story called "The Lurking Duck" by Scott Baker.

ED: Oh, yeah. I published it in *Omni*. Its problem was that it was exceptionally long. It was a novella. I don't remember how long it was originally. It's not that no one would take it because it was offensive. When I acquired it for *Omni*, Scott Baker and I had trimmed it to 11,200 words, because it was way, way too long. David Hartwell had talked about it for a few years, so I was happy to publish it, even in its truncated form. It's about a mechanical duck that swims in a lake and kills people, a predator, and a young girl. But it was a novella, a long novella, and that's why people turned it down, not because it wasn't a good story.

DS: Maybe it could have been expanded into a book.

ED: That was the problem then, not now. Now there's a market for novellas. So, yes, "The Lurking Duck" lurked for quite a few years before I ended up buying it for *Omni*. David eventually published the full-length version in *The Foundations of Fear*.

DS: As I recall, you stayed with *Omni* into its post-print life. Wasn't there about a year's worth of electronic issues that you edited?

ED: We continued publishing online for more than a year. When we started . . . Remember when AOL had a section on their website and they had weird stuff in the back end of their site someplace? I never understood how it worked or where the novellas published there were. Keith Ferrell got Ford or a different car company to fund six novellas. They were commissioned for a nice chunk of change, and they all ended up . . . somewhere . . . on AOL.

DS: I don't. I've actually never seen those electronic issues of *Omni*.

ED: Those stories were online, but they were not part of *Omni*. And they were not published in print. Although later a few were picked up for print publication. Silverberg wrote one. Jack Dann. Pat Cadigan, Dick Lupoff, Dan Simmons, and Michaela Roessner. I think I was able to acquire one final novella on *Omni*'s dime, one by Howard Waldrop that had a tiny, limited print edition. But as I said, I don't think this was actually the Internet. It was during *Omni*'s transition from print to digital.

DS: Do they still exist?

ED: They've either been reprinted by the authors or expanded into novels (in the case of Pat Cadigan's *Tea from an Empty Cup*).

DS: I've always had this feeling that unless it is archived properly, electronic publication is like skywriting.

ED: Yes, and no. What's frustrating is that once we created the *Omni* website, it could have made money from having all this original content online, but the sales and marketing people of General Media, the parent company, had no clue how to sell anything online. We had plenty of page impressions, so we probably *could* have sold advertising, but no one at the corporation knew how to do it.

DS: There was a least one later paper issue. I know, I have a copy.

ED: Pam Weintraub, Rob Killheffer, and Cory Powell (a science editor Pam knew) tried to publish a revived *Omni* for two or three issues, but we couldn't raise the money to keep it going.

DS: I remember one late issue of *Omni* that was actually on the newsstands.

ED: I commissioned a story by Maureen McHugh for it. Also, one by Nancy Kress, and another by Rich Larson, for the second issue, if I remember correctly.

DS: I've only seen one. And your career has mostly shifted to anthologies and horror since then.

ED: No, it hasn't. I acquire science fiction and fantasy, as well as horror short stories and novellas for Tor.com. In the past few years I've acquired sf novellas by Paul Cornell and Kelly Robson, and many fantasy novellas. I've published short sf by Michael Cassutt, Rich Larson, Nancy Kress, Genevieve Valentine, Lavie Tidhar, Paul McAuley, Nina Allan, and others. And plenty of fantasy and dark fantasy for the site as well.

DS: A question about horror. There is a quote I have been stealing for years and sometimes have heard attributed to you. Are you the person who said that the essence of a good horror story is that it "leaves you with an object of lasting contemplation"?

ED: Nope. Not me. Lasting contemplation?

DS: The idea is that a good horror story doesn't just say "Boo!" and go away. There is something that lingers.

ED: I never said it, but it's a good line.

DS: We can always say it was you. It might have been David Hartwell, but I thought it was you.

ED: No, definitely not me. What I have said about horror is that the difference between horror and dark fantasy is that horror rarely has a happy ending. A horror story, if it doesn't have a negative ending, has a neutral ending, and the person who has gone through the horror has experienced something that changes them. I think most horror has a negative ending. It's often nihilistic. Dark fantasy has a joy and exuberance to it. For example, the Sandman Slim novels by Richard Kadrey have a certain joy to them. The tone is very different from what I consider horror, which is bleak.

DS: I know from my much more limited experience that if you're commissioning new stories for an anthology, you can't publish a whole book of stories in which everybody dies at the end of every one.

ED: Everybody doesn't have to die for a story to be a horror story.

DS: But you do see a lot of those. If you're not careful you can end up with a book of stories in which everybody dies at the end.

ED: I've never noticed. I hope that's not the case in my anthologies. One interesting thing, though: Terri Windling and I were working on one of our YA anthologies, and we needed to solicit a few more stories. I realized as I started my line edit on the stories we'd bought so far that all the stories were first-person. *All* of them. So I contacted those who hadn't yet turned in their stories—like Garth Nix. I think I asked what point of view their story was going to be in and Garth responded, "Oh, you don't want first-person stories?" I laughed. I guess it's a YA thing. That's the only time point of view ever jumped out at me. You can jigger a story so that it doesn't come across as first-person, which is what Garth did. But that was an unsettling experience for me.

DS: I remember something Tappan King once told me about the *Twilight Zone* slush pile. He said that at least half of the stories could be summarized as "a man encounters the supernatural, then he dies."

ED: Right.

DS: Which is of course not very interesting after a while.

ED: There must be more going on in *any* story, or else I'll find it dull. Even if that's the frame, there must be other layers under the surface to keep the reader interested.

DS: Getting back to your distinction between dark fantasy and horror, where do we classify *Dracula*?

ED: *Dracula* to me is horror.

DS: But the good guys win.

ED: But they lose things—literally and figuratively.

DS: Some people die, yes.

ED: So it is not a happy ending, for some people. It's grim. They've learned that the world is horrible, that there are these vampire creatures that exist. So that's not dark fantasy. That's horror to me.

I don't read much dark fantasy. In fact, I have to distinguish between the two, because I don't want to publish dark fantasy in my *Best Horror of the Year*. I want to publish horror. Sometimes I read stories published as horror but in my opinion are not. I can't give you examples because I try to avoid those works. I intentionally put "blinders" on while reading for my best of the year in order to read what I *need* to read.

DS: There are people who argue that horror is anything published as horror, but obviously not.

ED: People can define it any way they want. I've given you my definition. They can agree with me or disagree. They're just wrong. [Laughs.] Kidding.

I don't understand the term "grimdark." I think I'd have to read more of what is referred to as grimdark in order to classify it. Then I'll judge whether it's horror or simply another type of dark fantasy.

DS: I think it means a very nasty sort of sword & sorcery, so that the Kane series of Karl Edward Wagner would be an example.

ED: Sword & sorcery isn't horror. There can be horrific things happening in dark fantasy. Being dark fantasy doesn't mean there are no horrific elements in the work. To me it is the final feeling that lingers, the overall tone by the end of the book.

DS: There are a couple great horror moments in *The Lord of the Rings*. I can think of one scene that is worthy of M. R. James.

ED: I still wouldn't consider the books horror.

DS: No. But doesn't all this have more to do with how a book is marketed?

ED: Maybe. Sometimes. But when I'm reading something I'm told is horror and it's not, I get annoyed—because as I said, I'm reading specifically for *The "Best Horror"* all the time. As a general reader I don't care. I love the Sandman Slim books and have happily read all of them. I've included them in my summary of the year in horror because I love them.

DS: Do you think it's possible to have funny horror?

ED: Yes, but it is extremely difficult to write.

DS: Robert Bloch did some of that.

ED: So often I just don't find what other readers consider humorous horror very funny. But Bloch could do it. Today, Jeff Strand writes humorous horror. Many of his stories don't work for me on that level, but occasionally they do. Again, that's just my opinion—I think what people find funny is pretty subjective. For me, the humor offsets the horror of the story.

DS: I think it can work if it starts out darkly humorous—

ED: And then gets darker and darker.

DS: Darker and darker until it is not funny.

ED: Sure. There is definitely that. The novella *Mr. Clubb and Mr. Cuff* by Peter Straub is a good example.

DS: Or else something isn't supposed to be funny, but it is.

ED: Do you mean because it is badly written?

DS: The best example I can think of comes from the movie of *The Legend of Hell House*, where they're setting up these refrigerator-sized computers in the living room and going through all this technobabble about ghosts and ectoplasm or whatever, and I realized we were just a hairline away from *Ghostbusters* there. It was potentially very funny. Of course *Hell House* came out first, in 1973, and *Ghostbusters* in 1984, so maybe I first saw *Hell House* much later than its initial release. But the computer scene in *Hell House* did strike me as being very close to the *Ghostbusters* sort of humor.

ED: There are many versions of that movie—which one are you referring to? Yes, but that's only because you're looking at it now from a time when computers are tiny, not when the movie was made. When it was made it was probably different.

DS: I was starting to snicker when I first saw it. I wasn't snickering at the size of the computers, in any case. I was snickering at the technobabble. I call to mind a comment Lovecraft made, to the effect that occult believers don't write good horror, because they take the supernatural for granted and reduce it to "professional" jargon.

ED: For people who believe in the occult, you mean? I think it is really difficult to write a successful supernatural novel. I think that the short story up to novella is easier. I am not a believer in the supernatural, so for me to suspend my disbelief for an entire four hundred pages is really, really tough, and I think it is really tough for an author to do that. It's been done, obviously, and done well by the best writers.

DS: I think of Ramsey Campbell making a career out of it, as has Stephen King. The whole horror boom of the '80s and '90s seemed to be novels.

ED: Yes, it was, but some of them were really bad.

DS: Have you read Grady Hendryx's *Paperbacks from Hell*?

ED: I have skimmed it. Some of the covers I was aware of. Others I was not. He does a whole survey of the paperbacks published during what—the '60s and '70s?

DS: He covers the period from the late '60s to the early '90s. His thesis is that the horror field as a commercial thing began with *Rosemary's Baby* and *The Exorcist* and *The Other* by Thomas Tryon, and it ended in a flood of serial killer novels in the early '90s.

ED: It's quite a display of book covers, so many of which are tacky. . . .

DS: He describes the clichés too. What I was impressed by was the astonishing number of books I had never heard of.

ED: I feel lucky that I never heard of some of them and so didn't have to read them. But, you know, the rash of serial killer novels and psychological horror novels were quite good. The trend began with *The Silence of the Lambs*, and a lot of mainstream writers were writing terrific serial killer novels, or psychological horror novels. Paul Theroux did one—*Chicago Loop*. Then there was *In the Cut* by Susanna Moore. The movie was with Meg Ryan and Mark Ruffalo. It wasn't exactly about a serial killer but it was about a killer. Moore had been lauded as a mainstream writer, and then she wrote this erotic, psycho-sexual horror novel and got slammed for it, but it was terrific. John Connelly, an Irish writer, started writing back then and his crime novels are ghost stories. I liked a lot of dark crime. James Lee Burke has moved into the supernatural realms for several of his more recent novels. For a while I was reading a lot of quirky crime. They weren't exactly horror, but

I felt I could justify including them because they were so weird—I figured my audience might appreciate those books. Like George Chesbro's series about "Mongo the Magnificent," a detective who happened to be a dwarf. Andrew Vachss's early novels like *Flood* and *Strega* were very good, but I eventually tired of his series. So there were writers experimenting, halfway falling into the horror category. There was a lot of fascinating cross-pollination going on between crime and horror—Joe R. Lansdale, the late Jack Ketchum, Joyce Carol Oates, are great examples of writers mixing those genres.

DS: We note now that the horror category has disappeared in most bookstores, inasmuch as there are still bookstores, and a good deal of horror is small press again.

ED: I disagree. Just because there are fewer bookstores carrying horror under the niche of "horror" doesn't mean tons of it isn't being published. Most mainstream publishers are publishing horror novels—they're just not necessarily called that. I get regular PR blasts from mainstream publishers about gothics and other dark fictions. As always, I need to judge whether these are dark fantasy are horror. This one is not for me. This one is for me. Like Isobel Cañas. Her first novel, *The Hacienda*, was very successful, and a second, *The Vampires of El Norte*, was recently published. Also Silvia Moreno-Garcia, Stephen Graham Jones, Clay McLeod Chapman, Christopher Golden, Elizabeth Hand, Danielle Trussoni, Ally Wilkes—their work is all being published by mainstream publishers. And for horror short fiction, of course, it's a golden age.

DS: We seem to have an incredible number of anthologies, and more magazines, mostly electronic, than anybody can count.

ED: Yes, I mentioned above. But not mostly electronic. There are plenty of print magazines publishing horror—I know—I read, or at least skim them. Actually I think there is less science fiction. There are science fiction imprints that are doing regular science fiction but not so many sf magazines—print or electronic.

DS: You probably have a better grasp of this than almost anybody, because of all the reading you have to do.

ED: Yup.

DS: So with all this reading, you must have made some exciting discoveries in the genre. Who are some of them?

ED: There are always wonderful new writers. In 2022 there were nine writers I've never published before. Some of the newer writers in *The Best Horror of the Year, Volume Fifteen* are Gemma Amor, Daniela Tomova, Andy Davidson, Jordan Shiveley, Luigi Musolino, Jacob Steven Mohr, and Charlie Hughes. Late last year I read the brilliant, shocking Irish novel *Where I End* by Sophie White. It's body horror, and I'm delighted to say it tied for the Shirley Jackson Award in the Best Novel category. I also loved *Sundial* by Catriona Ward and Sarah Gailey's *Just Like Home*. And *Maeve Fly* by C. L. Leede is a brilliant debut in 2023. So there are some excellent new writers being published in short and long categories.

DS: You posted a bunch of photos of yourself on Facebook recently, traveling around Europe. Does your work follow you on vacation?

ED: Yes, the friend I was traveling with couldn't understand why I had to be on e-mail all the time. But Twitter just erupted, and as a member of the board for the organization in question, I couldn't ignore it. I was gone for almost three weeks. While little flares aren't always dire, they still need to be addressed. I'm on two genre association boards, so, no, the responsibility of being "on call" never goes away. Also, as a freelancer, my work is not going to stop dead. Even if I only worked for one publisher, if one of my authors is having a problem that I can help with, I can't just ignore them.

DS: Does your backlog of reading follow you around too?

ED: I really had hoped to finish the summary for the current *Best Horror of the Year* before I left town, and I didn't. I *was* able to finish a few days after I got home. My final steps are to go through *Locus* and look at the books published in 2022 to ensure I didn't miss any horror publications. Then I edit my summary. While editing, I still had some last bits of reading to finish. Sometimes, at the last minute I'll read a story or poem that I can't resist, that's brilliant—in that case, I'll ask my editor if I can squeeze it into the book.

DS: Do you have a finite word limit? What would happen if at the last minute you did find something brilliant? Do you have to bump something out?

ED: I do have a finite limit. When I was co-editing *The Year's Best Fantasy and Horror* I acquired "Mr. Clubb and Mr. Cuff" by Peter Straub. Back then it was harder to count words accurately. Now I use Microsoft Word to count wordage, but then you had to estimate, and I was a notoriously lousy estimator. Peter's novella was much longer than I thought, so I had to cut two stories that I wanted for the book. One was by someone I had never heard of, whom I didn't know, and I don't think I had contacted them yet, so it was not a big deal. The other was by Dallas Mayr (a.k.a. Jack Ketchum), who was a friend, and he was really sweet about it. He was very understanding. But I never stopped feeling guilty.

The wordage might be different from year to year. It depends on my advance. At one point *The Best Horror of the Year* was up to 160,000 words, but then my advance was cut, so it went down to 130,000. However. It looks like it's crept back up to almost 160,000 words. I don't think my editor cares, although obviously it can't be too large a book, and I don't want to end up with no payment for myself.

DS: If it gets too large, the cover price of the book will go up.

ED: Right. Or . . . they could make the type smaller. [Laughs.] Then you'll need a little magnifying glass to read.

DS: I guess we can go to questions now. Anyone have any questions?

From audience: We always hear about what makes a good story or a good writer. What makes a good editor? What is the editor's job?

ED: If I'm working on an original anthology (editing reprint anthologies is different) my job is to push the writer to express what they intend to express in the story. If I love a story that's submitted to me but feel it needs a lot of revision, I'll work with the author on the manuscript before I commit to the work's acquisition. I'll ask questions—what's going on here? I don't understand this. I'll ask them to explain to me what they going on. And I might say to them: that isn't what's on the page. I try to help writers bring out the best in their story and make sure what they intend actually comes across, because you want the reader to "get" it. Once I acquire a story, I always give it a final line edit a few months before I need to turn the manuscript in to production. I go over it line by line. That is when I have more minor questions—but often a lot of them and/or suggestions such as "Did you mean to say that?" "Is that word/phrase intentional, or not?" "You've repeated this word or phrase too many times throughout the story," etc.

Someone else asked [Ellen is reading from the Zoom chat], could you talk about your editing with Terri Windling.

I worked with Terri on a number of books, and we loved working together.

For *The Year's Best Fantasy and Horror* we didn't collaborate at all. We each created our halves separately. We each had the same amount of words to fill. She covered fantasy, I covered horror. Jim Frenkel, as the packager, put our two halves together in an order he felt worked. Once in a while Jim told us we picked the same story, and when that happened, we each wrote a brief note explaining why we choose it for our half, and we split the wordage.

The six adult retold fairy tale anthologies were the first original anthologies on which we collaborated. Usually when you collaborate each editor gets one "free" story (that is, if the other person doesn't like it, you still buy it) and one free "no" (if one of you hates a story, you turn it down). Terri and I usually agreed on our choices, but once when we didn't, I used the story for a different anthology.

When co-editing anthologies, we divided up the list of writers we wanted to solicit work from and contacted them. I did a lot of the actual line editing, although Terri worked with the writers she knew better than I did. I kept track of the finances—I handled all the payments and royalties, something I still do. Terri wrote all the excellent, comprehensive introductions to each book and the further reading sections.

Then we co-edited the four mythic anthologies, and three middle-grade fairy tale anthologies; also *Queen Victoria's Book of Spells* and *Salon Fantastique*, the latter a non-theme fantasy anthology.

If Terri had the time and energy, and wasn't busy with her own projects, I'd wouldn't mind collaborating on another anthology with her.

However, I do prefer editing solo anthologies, so that the contents are all my taste. The problem with every collaboration is that each editor must compromise, even if just a bit.

DS: Okay, I have a question for you: After all this extensive exposure to stories, have you ever felt the temptation to write one yourself?

ED: No. I have nothing I'd want to write about. I am a decent photographer—I have an excellent sense of framing and seeing what looks good, but I could not draw or paint to save my life. I believe photography and editing emanate from a different part of the brain than painting and drawing and writing. I can only work with something that already exists. I am unable to make up something out of nothing.

DS: I am surprised. Most editors I know are writers or would-be writers.

ED: Gordon Van Gelder wrote one story years ago and never did again. He realized that he didn't want to do it, or couldn't.

Shawna McCarthy, I think, might have written or co-written one story, and that was it. I think Beth Meacham wrote or co-wrote a story once. But yes, in sf certainly, there is a tradition of the editor/writer. Richard Christian Matheson and I had lunch in New York City one day many years ago and he asked, "How can you be an editor if you don't write?" and I responded that "I'm a better editor *because* I don't write, because I am not trying to impose my writing style on you, or my ideas. I have no skin in this game. I am trying to get you to make your story better. I am not going to rewrite your work."

Years ago, at *Omni,* an agent sent me a submission. Another writer, who was also an editor, had told me that the writer was hard to work with. I mentioned this to the agent who said, "No, they're not." Then I talked to the writer, and it turned out that the writer/editor wanted to rewrite their work, and that was why they were "hard to deal with."

I don't know how a writer/editor does it. You'd have to turn off the writerly part of your brain, I'd think, in order to edit well. Don't you?

DS: My feeling is that the writing part can inform the editing, and it can help you understand what the writer is going through, and maybe suggest solutions. But I as an editor would never force anything on a writer, and say, "Rewrite the story this way," or, worse yet, do it myself. Horace Gold, the editor of *Galaxy,* was notorious for that. Many times writers would read their own stories in the magazine and not know how they were going to turn out. It was said of Horace that he could take a mediocre story and turn it into a good story, but he could also take a great story and turn it into a good story.

ED: That's too bad.

DS: He was much too heavy-handed.

ED: That's where the questions come in. I don't want to impose my view on a writer. I want to know what they're attempting to do in the story. I've gone through multiple rewrites once in a while, although not too often. I remember I was working with Kelly Robson on her great story "A Human Stain," which, once published, won a Nebula. After two rewrites I said, "I don't understand what's going on. Why don't you tell me?" And once she did, I realized that what Kelly thought was on the page was not. The story needed major revision at that point because she hadn't expressed clearly enough what was happening. Eventually we were both happy with the story, although there were still a few unexplained bits in the story—visual cues or clues. But we were both afraid that if she made things too explicit, much of the mystery would fall away. Sometimes you and your author go over one manuscript so many times that neither of you are certain if the story works. Happily "A Human Stain" worked fine for most readers.

DS: Thinking more about writer/editors, I recall how Michael Moorcock practically wrote whole issues of *New Worlds,* but I think that sometime the writer/editor's job is to fill in the missing brick.

ED: For me it is to get the *author* to fill in the missing brick/s. I don't want to do it myself.

I generally don't commission stories, I *solicit* them. If you commission a piece of work, you have an obligation to either buy and publish it or give the author a "kill fee." I commissioned eleven series of themed short-shorts (now called flash fiction) for *Omni*—almost 50 stories—and I published all but one of them. I paid the author a kill fee for the one rejected story. On a panel once, Karl Edward Wagner claimed that if he was asked for a story, the editor was under an obligation to buy that story, whether they liked it or not, whether it worked for the venue or not. That's utter bullshit and I was shocked when he said it. If an editor is required to take every submission (including those stories you "solicited") you'll be a really lousy editor. One of the most important jobs of an editor is to make choices as to what to publish. If something doesn't work, or doesn't meld with the project, it's the editor's responsibility to turn it down.

DS: There must be some prima donna authors.

ED: Not many. The problem is that when editing a reprint anthology there are writers I won't/can't buy stories from—not because I don't like their stories or that they're difficult to work with but because getting permission from their agent, estate (if they're no longer alive), or book publisher (whatever entity controls the rights) takes too much energy, time, and/or money. I will no longer ask to reprint Stephen King's stories because even if I could get permission for English-language print rights, one has to acquire foreign rights individually and e-rights may not be available. If I want to use a story in an anthology, I need all those rights in one bundle.

DS: The kind of prima donna I am thinking of would be like Heinlein later in his career. He made it clear that if you ever rejected anything from him, you would never get another submission from him. A lot of people let him go.

ED: That's calling his bluff.

DS: There is a reason he stopped writing for John Campbell. Campbell rejected *Starship Troopers*. So he never submitted anything to *Astounding* again.

ED: Well, at *Omni* we (unfortunately) published an excerpt from *The Number of the Beast,* which was awful.

DS: I actually saw that in manuscript, I will have you know.

ED: Obviously we did, too. It was shortly after I was hired. I read some of it and I thought it awful.

DS: I can tell you something funny about that. The agent was running an auction, so the excerpt that ran in *Omni* was submitted to George Scithers at *Asimov's*. We all read it, and what I wrote on the index card was, "I wouldn't pay 2 cents a word for this." George declined to bid, which I think was wise. At some point you can't be in awe of the name. You have to go for the quality of the story.

ED: Right; acquiring it would not have been my choice, but this was early in *Omni*'s existence, and the Gucciones wanted big sf names in the magazine to help gain credibility with genre readers. Over the next couple of years we did have to publish other (let's just say) disappointing excerpts. I've always hated excerpts in any publication—I don't see the point.

DS: I think Ben Bova was fiction editor then. But, yeah, it was awful. Fred Pohl once said that if something was by Heinlein, even if it was bad, people would want to read it. He knew that *Farnham's Freehold* was awful, but he serialized it anyway, in *Worlds of If*. Because he bought that, he got *The Moon Is a Harsh Mistress*. Hopefully you don't have to make that kind of choice, where you have to put up with something awful by a writer in hopes that you will get something better later.

ED: Not any more. But I always thought they were/are a waste of limited space. I just wanted to publish original stories.

DS: A bit more generally, on the subject of writing, what advice do you have for writers, other than don't quit your day job?

ED: *Don't* quit your day job. Keep writing. Try to make time to write regularly, but don't hit yourself over the head if you can't write every day. Just *try*. And submit your work. Don't sit on any one project forever. It's good to rewrite but don't over-rewrite.

If you're in a workshop, you must be able to trust your fellow workshoppers and judge whether what they say about your work makes sense and is helpful. If you disagree with them all the time, then their critiques will not help you.

DS: We have a workshop at Philcon. I run it. I have a regular crew who will critique the five or six stories we get, and hopefully that does some good.

ED: I taught Clarion West several times, and a problem is that in most workshops where I participate, I'm only ever seeing the first draft of a story. As an editor, I don't see generally receive first draft submissions; I get a polished manuscript as a submission. I've finally realized that although I can advise students on the business side of publishing, I don't know how much I can help make their writing better. A story written a few days previously—specifically for a workshop—is unlikely to be in its final form, and that's not what I work with in my job. And teaching a week-long workshop and interacting with 17+ students daily is exhausting—physically and emotionally. After every workshop, I'd promise myself that I wouldn't teach again. But five or six years later I'd be asked back and I'd say yes, having forgotten that promise. I haven't been asked for several years now, and I'm relieved.

DS: My feeling about workshops is that if someone shows no improvement over about ten years, then you can give up. But I have seen miraculous transformations after a very long time, when somebody suddenly gets it and their stories start getting good.

ED: Yes, that happens. And there are stories that come out of workshops that are brilliant at first light (e.g., Ted Chiang's first story, "Tower of Babylon," which I subsequently published in *Omni,* was sent to me by Tom Disch, who read it at Clarion.)

Question from audience: Have you ever had a story that you loved but you could not print because it did not fit the theme?

ED: Oh, yes, but not often. When I edit a theme anthology I send guidelines as to what I'm looking for and what I don't want, and the writers I solicit usually send me work that fits the theme.

I intentionally keep my themed anthologies as broad as I can. I encourage the solicited writers to push against the theme. As long as I can personally reconcile a story I love to the theme, I'll take the story.

DS: The one advantage of doing a magazine rather than an anthology is that you don't have to do themes if you don't want to.

ED: That's why I love acquiring short fiction and novellas for Tor.com. I prefer not to do theme anthologies, but I have no choice because they sell better than non-theme anthologies.

DS: Neil Gaiman brought out an anthology that was just called *Stories*. That's because he's Neil Gaiman.

ED: I wonder how well it actually sold, particularly considering how high the advance likely was.

DS: It was marketed as a Neil Gaiman book. Anybody else would need another marketing angle.

ED: I've edited several non-themed anthologies, and they haven't done as well as my themed ones.

DS: I think that *Alternate Historical Vampire Cat Detectives* is only a matter of time.

[Datlow laughs.]

DS: I actually have a publisher interested in that, so I may be able to do it. I suspect it's going to be silly.

ED: Okay.

DS: What is the most unlikely anthology theme you can think of that actually works?

ED: Of my own books?

DS: Yes. Or anybody else's. *Alternate Kennedys* was pretty weird.

ED: In order to put together a good narrow-themed anthology, the editor would need to be extra careful to acquire stories different enough in tone and voice to ensure variety. I've seen at least one anthology of stories only about Count Dracula, and the anthology had a feeling of sameness throughout. That's why I think it's better to broaden the theme to include different vampires, or even to vampirism (which is what I've done multiple times) with only one or two stories featuring Dracula himself.

DS: There was an anthology of alternate Beatles stories.

ED: Was it any good and did it do well?

DS: I don't know. It was a small press. Ian Strock published it. Right now I am editing an anthology called *Cold War Cthulhu*. I am getting a lot of stories about Russian spies.

ED: Then you must discourage the writers who haven't yet handed in stories from writing on that subject. You've got to just come out and tell them: no more spies.

DS: I require them to give me a hint first of what they propose to write about, so I don't get eight stories about Khrushchev banging his shoe in the U.N.

ED: That's what I did for my Poe-inspired anthology. I asked the writers to tell me in advance what Poe work they planned to use for inspiration. Although I received a few pieces inspired by the same story or poem, I knew in advance that the writers I chose to work with would each write very different stories. And they did. The most unusual inspiration was Glen Hirshberg using a news article written by Poe about a rampaging buffalo, which pleased me greatly, as who today has read, or even heard of this article? Writers are inventive, when they choose to be.

On the other hand, for *When Things Get Dark*, my Shirley Jackson anthology, I deliberately asked the writers to *avoid* being influenced by any specific work by Jackson. Instead, I wanted stories using some of her themes and her tone.

DS: For the writer that is often the challenge, to find something that no one else has taken.

ED: Yes.

DS: We're out of time. Thanks for being with us, Ellen.

Sacred Scares

Géza A. G. Reilly

FIONA SNAILHAM, ed. *Holy Ghosts: Classic Tales of the Ecclesiastical Uncanny*. London: British Library, 2023. 320 pp. £9.99 ($16.99) tpb. ISBN: 9780712354134.

As might be guessed from the subtitle, *Holy Ghosts* is an anthology of supernatural tales, usually but not always ghost stories, told within a religious frame of reference. These tales almost universally spring from a Christian worldview, and they are all ably told—with a few standouts and a few that land with proverbial thuds. What is most notable about this anthology is its theme. It is rare, I think, for an explicitly religious theme to be used in gathering stories for a modern volume, and that rarity adds *Holy Ghosts* an aura of charm all on its own.

What if the reader is not themselves religious, you might ask? I frankly think that this is a meaningless question. One does not have to be a materialist to appreciate Lovecraft's stories of titanic, but nevertheless *material*, alien beings lurking on the fringes of an otherwise atheist universe. The same can be said for the stories within *Holy Ghosts*—and other religious-themed stories besides. It does not matter if ghosts spring from Catholic soil (though, insofar as I am aware, the existence of ghosts is not accepted by the Catholic church); they can haunt us all the same.

And haunt us they do! As with *Night's Black Agents*, reviewed in this issue, *Holy Ghosts* opens with a strong introduction that points intriguingly at what each of the stories that follow suggests regardless of the action of their various plots. "Spectral apparitions suggest that holy settings are not always able to provide [. . .] protection," Snailham writes. "Spirits of those who have passed reveal holy sites as the setting of horrifying deaths, and malevolent phantoms threaten the safety of those visiting hallowed ground." The flip side, of course, is that the existence of those same spirits suggests that salvation, perhaps even redemption, is *possible* if not currently within reach. It is within the space of that tension between terror and transcendence that *Holy Ghosts* thrives.

The majority of the eleven stories within *Holy Ghosts* come to us from the nineteenth century; only three are twentieth-century products, and of those three only one feels like a truly modern work. Sadly, that is the capstone story for the anthology: "The Cathedral Crypt" by John Wyndham, dating to 1935. Although Wyndham's story is ably written, it is a bit thin and possesses little to grip the reader in terms of characterization, plot, or even atmosphere. Other, similar clunkers are thankfully few on the ground. Sheridan Le Fanu's "The Sexton's Adventure" is an amusing little piece, but it is a bit too twee for my liking—especially since it takes pride of place as the first story in the anthology, thus leading the reader into the whole with more of an O. Henry twist than a Jamesian burst of fear. (M. R. James is, of course, present in the anthology via his strong, but not iconic, "The Stalls of Barchester Cathedral" [1910].) Similarly, Ada Buisson's "A Story Told in a Church" (1867) is a fun but obvious affair that leans a bit too heavily into its nested narrative structure, and E. Nesbit's "Man-Size in Marble" (1887) is capably written but telegraphs its climactic twist so much that one's neck hurts during the reading.

Thankfully, the standouts in *Holy Ghosts* more than make up for the less affective affairs. Ellen Price's "The Parson's Oath" (1855) is a quasi-romance story that deals effectively with the plight of women in the period and hints toward the terrible truth of eternal existence plaguing wronged spirits. Elizabeth Gaskell's "The Poor Clare" (1856) is a fine tale of adventure, wrongdoing, and eventual redemption wrapped up in explicitly Christian contexts. Equally, Robert Hichens's "The Face of the Monk" (1897) comes at the same themes of evil and saintly good from a different direction, resulting in a wonderful ending that is as strangely happy as it is satisfying. The high-water mark in *Holy Ghosts* is, however, Margueritte Merington's "An Evicted Spirit," (1899) which is a ghost story told from the point of view of the ghost. While such an idea might seem hackneyed when described, Merington's tale is one of the most effective, poignant ghost stories I have ever read, and it alone makes the anthology worthy of a purchase.

Overall, *Holy Ghosts* is a charming read. It is rarely frightening, but it is often interesting in how each author approaches the very ideas he or she plays with. The metaphysical reality of an immortal spirit; the blasphemous nature of evil acts; the potentially transitory nature of the sacred; the vulnerability of the mortal—all these are at issue within the anthology's boards, and they are all effectively handled by the whole. Even if the reader is a non-believer in religious matters, there is much to be enjoyed in *Holy Ghosts*. After all, we all, to one degree or other, know of the existence of evil and good (even if we parse those terms in particular ways). Who among us would not be moved if it were demonstrated that acts bearing those labels could have echoes far beyond the impacts they have in the moment of their expression? That, ultimately, is the thrust of promise and peril in *Holy Ghosts*, and it is one that is well worth considering.

Crossing the Void
Michael D. Miller

MATT CARDIN. *Journals, Volume 2: 2002–2022*. Seattle: Sarnath Press, 2023. 306 pp. $16.95 tpb. ISBN: 979-8850409944.

> I walk a fine line in my innermost thoughts and attitudes, and I don't always walk it well. It is the line between embracing wholeness, purity, and light, and encouraging darkness.
> —MATT CARDIN

So begins the second and final volume of Matt Cardin's journals documenting two decades of spiritual awakening on the writer's path from 2002 to 2022. With nearly triple the time span of the eight years of Volume 1, the journals continue to expand the philosophical examinations of the Western and Eastern traditions, implications of a personal religious background in the foreground of "cosmic theology," and further explorations of the demon muse. But this volume sharply focuses on a growing awareness of questioning existence itself, who or what we really are, how do we know, and why bother doing anything at all. Due to the subjectivity of the journals, I thought the best review would be to interview the writer directly. So I sat down with Matt Cardin via *Zoom* on October 18 in the prime of horror season to take a deep delve behind *Journals, Volumes 1 and 2*.

Matt's initiation into the weird and horrific through Lovecraft to Ligotti is familiar to many of us born in a certain era (circa 1970). Matt began by sharing an orientation to speculative fiction especially fantasy, science fiction, and horror with a commonality of how it all works. Like many of us at ages eight to fourteen, fantasy was the genre of choice—fantasy being Tolkien, Moorcock, Saberhagen, Rosenberg, Brooks, with *Dungeons and Dragons* factoring heavily into those authors.

We can all recall where or when we first heard the name of Lovecraft. For Matt it came from an early 80s "D&D explosion" book—*Dicing with Dragons*. The book mentioned another game that served as an initiation rite to Lovecraftian works, the *Call of Cthulhu* role-playing game, noting that Marvel comics also provided many Lovecraftian troupes. All in all, Matt was primed for Lovecraft before ever reading him. The game itself coalesced many ideas already formed in the psyche. Then followed a quick dive into the Ballantine Michael Whelan covers Lovecraft anthologies to cement it. Reading Lovecraft confirmed all. This followed by interest in the man himself when discovering de Camp's *Lovecraft: A Biography* at the county library in 1986–87. At that point Lovecraft became a drug. "An emotional and philosophical education in cosmic horror for someone already primed in psyche and soul to receive it." Matt combined this with his evangelical background and grasp of religion, namely the aspect of "disturbing the universe" taken from Don Burleson's critical work.

During college Cardin's self-imposed side-curriculum was Lovecraft criticism (with the work of Schweitzer, Burleson, Lévy, and Joshi) and backed by the cinema of the time (*Re-Animator, Alien, The Thing*), followed by immersion in S. T. Joshi's corrected texts for Arkham House. The Ligotti segue was philosophical and creative. A minor in philosophy, the study of Eastern religion, Alan Watts, Zen, etc. and terrible bouts with sleep paralysis in 1994 led Matt to write "Teeth," eventually published on *Ligotti Online* by Jon Padgett. This was prior to discovering Ligotti, but comparisons led to reading *Grimscribe* and finding the incantatory writing almost too powerful to believe. Yet such a nihilistic, pessimistic, Lovecraftian, cosmic horror state lead naturally to Ligotti. It was a "complete organic move. Ligotti is the modern distillation of all that was best in Lovecraft. A subjective and arguable view, yet I stand by it . . ."

MM: Least we forget Edgar Allan Poe, there is a presence of weirdness only perceivable by the narrator (and the reader by default) separate from what is happening in the narrative, and I believe in your journals you called this "the experience of first-personhood and the nature of subjectivity." How important is this to anyone who wants to write authentically in the tradition of Poe, Lovecraft, and Ligotti?

MC: It is non-negotiably important. The depth and possible perturbations and disturbances and alterations of perspective of mundane reality that occur in first-person subjectivity are the most important aspects of weird fiction and horror. Ligotti's "The Red Tower" is a powerful example, essentially plotless, characterless, a brilliant exercise in experimental fiction, and yet it is told from the viewpoint of a deranged subjectivity of its own, and it affects the reader's subjectivity in interesting ways. It is a transformative reading experience of prose fiction. Both for the reader and the narrative viewpoint of these stories, the questioning, the undermining, the overturning, the warping, and the disturbing of first-personhood is primary in weird fiction in a way that it is not for any other type of fiction.

MM: The idea of journaling itself seems connected to that. It is a first-person account of the experiences of the writer. Writing is not just something to do for money or publication or fame; it's actually more real than that. The struggle of relating that to existence is clear in your journals. What are your thoughts on the role of the journal for writers of the weird and horror tradition?

MC: One, it is important in the lives of the authors themselves. But also in the entirety of the Gothic tradition journals and diaries play a central role. For the lives of the writers, and I mentioned this in my final entry to the journal, in retrospect, journals conceal as much as they reveal. My own journals often present an obverse of what anyone observing my actual life may perceive. I would often turn to the journal to engage with things not possible in my outer life. A person's subjectivity is then called to the fore in honestly writing to oneself without thought of anyone else simply for the purpose of writing. It is one of the most active ways to become aware of the nature of one's subjectivity. That can certainly be effective in the artform that uses such subjectivity.

MM: On that subjectivity, many Lovecraft or Ligotti stories seem as if they were written as if no one else would ever read them. They have that sort of power to it. Are there any journals by other writers that you theoretically wish you could read where we don't have them readily available or published?

MC: The journal of Thomas Ligotti, although *The Conspiracy against the Human Race* comes close to approaching that. Yet his own private writing may be different, or not. As I pointed out, the sense of managing to do that impossible thing as Poe famously spoke of writing an ultimate, and ultimately impossible, book whose title would be *My Heart Laid Bare*. It seems Ligotti actually has managed to write that. He really has put himself out there with anti-natalism and his tortured persona to the disdain of many readers who are too comfortable in their shallow reality.

MM: In your journals I noted a struggle between consciousness and annihilation. The idea of who we think we are and the annihilation of that idea. That may be the ultimate horror in the sense that maybe journals of that level are more terrifying than any work of fiction can ever be. Especially true when we consider this is happening to the writer, giving it an almost equal feel to the confrontation with the unknown or fear of annihilation these stories produce. Where does the demon muse fit into that process? It is one thing to consider these things in a story, but a whole other matter when they are really happening to the author.

MC: The demon muse has two halves to it. The demon, the thing the prods you, the fiery, primal energy that is moving you and the muse, the channel to the gods or the archetypes or realm of the ideas, the imaginal realm that provides the source materials. That right there is an intra-psychic phenomenon like being connected to another intelligence. It highlights, it foregrounds, it calls out things about the nature of personal identity and reality and subjectivity that widen the sense of identity. So that fear of personal annihilation becomes recontextualized. What do you mean by "I"? What do you mean by my "self"? What do you mean that "I" or my "self" might be wiped out of existence? "I" is actually bigger or smaller than you think. Your ego "I" is swamped from above and below from ideas of your wider identity, but it feels like "not you." Call it the unconscious identity, but all that does is put a name on something that is obscuring the fact that it is a mystery. You can also say "I" is wider. The demon muse is actually "I" in the wider sense. Connecting back to annihilation, it is really a fear of the personal ego being annihilated, either as a psychological fact or mystical experience. The wider self sinks into the idea of being itself. It changes it. The demon muse is a link to a wider sense of identity than appears to be connected to the conscious self. If the conscious self goes away would the deeper one still be there?

MM: At that point we are going even beyond weird fiction. Most of the stories end at that point where the annihilation of whatever, the self in this case, happens. That is the horrific moment or terminal climax for the narrative. The demon muse continues beyond these apocalyptic realizations. Is the demon muse akin to an ability or power?

MC: I would say no. The demon muse is a layer of identity. An ability would be some quality that "you" as a separate being have. The demon muse has you. You are a quality of the demon muse. You are an emanation down the chain of being from the demon muse so to speak.

MM: Is that the realization then? It is you more than you think it is?

MC: Right. It is closer to you than you think you are.

MM: It is bigger than us. And bigger than weird fiction. You mentioned the "self as a literary construction." Through that questioning you arrived at "why bother?" That is a huge void to cross and is revisited time after time in your journals. When we think of worldly developments like A.I. replicating fiction at this point, there could be a day when the commercial sense of what fiction is could be annihilated by A.I. One thing it could never do is experience the process of that journal, forcing yourself to face the difficult questions on the road to discovery and annihilation on your own. Maybe eventually the journal will be the popular choice over fiction.

MC: A.I.-produced writing raises the question of who it is for. It is not written by anyone. Language model A.I.'s are not sentient. It really is like the infinite number of monkeys tapping keys and eventually producing something a language apparatus model could eventually understand. It is based on algorithmic rules. If you have a world full of people reading essays written by A.I.'s, what subjectivity are they hooking into? What is the point of the writing or the reading? It is pure distraction. There is no person. There is nothing channeled through a perspective because there was no perspective that wrote it. If the journal is the most pointed, pure, personal form of writing, the core of what human writing will need to be going forward resonates with me, because that form of writing where an actual sentient being is using writing to figure out the mystery of sentience, the mystery of identity, the mystery of first-personhood, the cradle in which he or she has been ensconced from birth, that can only be produced by that person. It is proprietary writing unique to each individual and never invokes the question of who is writing this or why is it being written or why read it. It is the antithesis of that by its very nature. So yeah, I agree with you, with writing produced on a cheap scale by these things, ultra-personal writing by actual people will take on a new premium.

MM: The last refuge of subjectivity would be in the journal. Part of your current work seems to be geared towards teaching and learning. Is that the goal of *The Living Dark* blog?

MC: Yeah. From 2009 to 2011 I ran *The Demon Muse* blog, the culmination of that exploration of the inner genius. Most of my entries became my ebook, *A Course in Demonic Creativity*. It is free at my mattcardin.com website. After 2022 I decided I wanted to write a Substack blog/newsletter, like my prior blog, *The Teeming Brain* (2006–22). *The Teeming Brain* was about channeling the multiverse of ideas. *The Living Dark* is all that with a focus on creativity. My journey into a "non-dual" view of existence has intensified over the last five or six years, while it has been there for twenty or thirty years. *The Living Dark* fuses the demon muse sense of creativity with A) we are living in an ascendant apocalyptic age, and B) living out the implications of the non-dual viewpoint. This is the understanding that one's self is a construct, a fiction. Your identity right now is a spacious field of awareness, presence, in which your whole idea of your presence in the wider world is just a show, an outflow, a configuration of shapes. We are all the same . . . the same one, being. Some find it fascinating; others find it stupid. But talking about it is another matter. I theorized about it in thirty years of journaling. But my awakening to it unfolded over that last five years. The sensory perceptions of the world around me are the contents of awareness. And if you are aware of something, you are not it. You are whatever is aware of it. That is the subjectivity. So what is the subject? That seems to be nothing to the conscious mind. The essence is that we are one thing witnessing projections of the one thing. This obviously ties into all the issues in weird fiction we've been talking about.

MM: Yes. That easily carries over to the cosmic quality of weird fiction as well. Last question. We are in the middle of October season. Is there anything you do to celebrate the mood and atmosphere? Any films or music you might traditionally visit?

MC: I might read a story or two from Bradbury's *October County,* but I don't read much fiction anymore. I can actually get as much joy holding Bradbury's book and leafing through it as I can from actually reading it. Sometimes I'll listen to music by Goblin or Rob Zombie. I may reread some Lovecraft or Ligotti. I just discovered last year that every October Sirius XM has a pop-up station called *Scream*, "your station for Halloween." It's full of weird unexplained soundscapes, wordless stories or fully written audio plays, lots of horror movie soundtrack music. Driving home today they were playing the score from the 1963 version of *The Haunting*. Yesterday was the soundtrack to John Carpenter's *The Fog*. I savored it. But really, lots of these things feel more distant than they used to be. It used to feel great when my emotions were inflamed in autumn by all those books and movies and all that music. But speaking from a non-dual viewpoint, trying to import all that can wear out the notional "you." The thing you are seeking is not actually in the things you are seeking it through. I am much more interested in a more primary experience of happiness now.

The journals are not the final word of Matt Cardin. You can continue crossing the void with Matt by subscribing to his blog, *The Living Dark*, at thelivingdark.net. Sarnath Press has done us all a favor by publishing these journals, and if you are willing to take the plunge into the confrontation with the annihilation of the self as (the notional) "I" did, the journals are a rewarding read that will linger for a long time to come.

New Ways to Dread the Holidays

Dave Felton

ELLEN DATLOW, ed. *Christmas and Other Horrors: A Winter Solstice Anthology*. London: Titan Books, 2023. 448 pp. $27.99 hc. ISBN: 9781803363264.

> There'll be scary ghost stories and tales of the glories of Christmases long, long ago.
> —"It's the Most Wonderful Time of the Year"

Most listeners who grew up with Andy Williams's 1963 song in their heads during the holidays probably associate only Charles Dickens with Christmas ghosts, but readers of *Dead Reckonings* are sure to be more familiar with the Victorian tradition of telling ghostly tales around the hearth during long mid-winter nights. It is a literary tradition that has been carried on from Sir Walter Scott and Elizabeth Gaskell to M. R. James and Algernon Blackwood, and with the publication of *Christmas and Other Horrors* by Titan Books, Ellen Datlow has gathered eighteen stories by contemporary writers of weird fiction that look to add a new chill to the season. As the award-winning editor of so many anthologies, not the least being the ongoing *Best Horror of the Year* by Night Shade Books, Datlow is without doubt most experienced and capable of putting together a collection of tales based upon the holiday season and all it entails. It does not disappoint, as there is something for everyone—Christmas, Hanukkah, Kwanzaa, Festivus, the New Year, the Epiphany, and other nameless or forgotten holidays humans have celebrated around the Winter Solstice, the shortest day of the year, and also the longest, darkest night; perfect for these tales of dread.

The collection opens with "The Importance of a Tidy Home" by Christopher Golden, a Bram Stoker Award–winning novelist also known for his collaborations with Mike Mignola, the creator of Hellboy. In the city of Salzburg a pair of homeless men follow the *schnabelperchten*, creatures in Austrian folklore that visit homes on the Eve of the Epiphany, January 5th, to inspect the cleanliness and order of the city inhabitants at the start of the new year. The transients, without having homes themselves, seem to be above any risk of judgment and consequence, and so become witnesses of this visitation and the consequences of not keeping a clean room. It would be easy for the reader to envision the creatures, eyeless beaked faces with bloody scissors in hand, rendered by Mignola at some later date, and there is a sense that Golden's story treads in that world of monster comic books, of Old World legends that come to life on one magic night a year. And there are some witches and vampires in the pages that follow, but most of the monsters in this anthology look decidedly human: the holidays bring out the best in people, and also their worst.

Keep a clean house or risk a visit from the *schnabelperchten*. Also, children, you'd better be good because Santa is watching and judging, rewarding the good, and possibly punishing the bad. That punishing aspect lends a sinister aspect to the Santa legend, around which Benjamin Percy spins his story "The Ones He Takes." A child is concerned about following proper Christmas etiquette, and is sure to leave out milk and cookies. "I don't want to make him mad . . . I don't want to be on the naughty list," he says, and pleads with his father to open the chimney flue so good ol' Saint Nick can enter the house. But what if the big man in red is amoral, above good and evil, and has needs of his own? What if Santa takes instead of gives? A holiday-themed horror anthology can be expected to have its share of the Santa specter, but Datlow wisely steered away and chose only this one, which has an undercurrent critique of capitalism, consumerism, and labor. The horrors!

Alma Katsu's "His Castle" is written around the Welsh tradition of Mari Lwyd, or the gray mare, which we are given to believe is derived from The Feast of the Ass, a holiday that commemorates the biblical story of Joseph and Mary's flight into Egypt, and the donkey that carried that holy family. In a similar fashion, the London couple of this story decides to get away from the city for the holidays to visit the small village of their childhoods, and come up against charlatans parading festively with a hobby horse topped by a horse's skull, with suspiciously ill-intent. But all is not as it seems in this ghost story: "Something besides familial obligation draws us back to the ancestral sod." It is a sentiment found in Lovecraft's own Christmas story "The Festival," that sense of obligation to gather with family for the holidays, to eat, drink, and make merry, or just become reconnected with kin. As events unfold, the reader learns of the pre-Christian roots of Mari Lwyd and what it might mean for ghosts to return home for the holidays.

Unsurprisingly, many of the stories in this anthology deal with families during the holidays, often a stressful time of year, and the pain of relationships made more keen during what should be a festive season. In the story "Return to Bear Creek Lodge," Tananarive Due writes of her characters' intergenerational trauma, set against Christmas and Kwanzaa's principle of unity and togetherness. A grandmother lingers before death, the end of her life timed with the end of the year, the coldest and darkest season. The dying woman is hated and feared by her daughter and grandson after a history of abuse, but these feelings are countered by rage as well: against death, guilt, and family secrets. Instead of a peaceful holiday family gathering, there are nightmares, and fear poisons everyone during their stay at the lodge.

In an anthology of fiction, the best stories are often the ones that make you forget you're reading an anthology at all, so captivating and convincing they are, and finishing the story makes you wish there were another by that same voice. Such was the case when reading Nadia Bulkin's "All the Pretty People," which occurs at a Festivus party; Festivus being an alternative to an overly commercialized Christmas, and a holiday that entered into pop culture through a 1997 episode of *Seinfeld*. Its celebration as a secular holiday in this story is at first felt done in irony and fun, but it soon becomes apparent there is a tragic seriousness in each of the guests, flaws that each contribute to a pervading sadness among them, and to the absence of one particular friend. The story is culturally self-aware enough to capture a moment in time and an age of young adulthood, and smart enough to not explain references and name-drops.

Another immensely satisfying read is the final story, "After Words" by John Langan. It is written as dialogue between a couple engaged in pillow talk, as the narrator relates a tale of a long-lost high school sweetheart and vigorous ritual sex magic. If you're a person who has loved and lost someone, you might speculate in what ways, if any, the past might meet the present, how one could re-encounter or re-engage with someone seemingly long gone. It is human speculation and fancy, and the way the story is teased during a couple's tender moment, playful and contented with each other, lulls the reader into the story's own spell, broken only when you realize the ghost is already next to you.

Each of the eighteen tales is followed by brief author notes that provide some insight into its creation. Perhaps it was a family trip to a foreign country, a weird ornament seen hanging in a store window, books of myths and folklore and traditional holiday recipes. Some writers had social issues in mind that simmered under the fiction—climate change, homelessness—and the mental exhaustion of it. A few listened to music, watched YouTube, walked the dog, or simply dreamed their stories. Together, these authors and their stories comprise a fresh and diverse holiday horror anthology that will have you dread the season in new ways.

About the Contributors

Ramsey Campbell is an English horror fiction writer, editor, and critic who has been writing for well over fifty years. He is frequently cited as one of the leading writers in the field. His website is www.ramseycampbell.com.

Dave Felton is a copy editor at Cadabra Records and an illustrator of weird fiction.

Alex Houstoun is a co-editor of *Dead Reckonings*. He has published *Copyright Questions and the Stories of H. P. Lovecraft*, available by contacting him at deadreckoningsjournal@gmail.com.

S. T. Joshi is a widely published literary and cultural critic and the author of *The Weird Tale* (1990), *I Am Providence: The Life and Times of H. P. Lovecraft* (2010), *Unutterable Horror: A History of Supernatural Fiction* (2012), and many other volumes. He has edited the work of H. P. Lovecraft, Ambrose Bierce, Lord Dunsany, H. L. Mencken, Leslie Stephen, and other writers.

Katherine Kerestman is the author of *Lethal* (PsychoToxin Press, 2023) and *Creepy Cat's Macabre Travels: Prowling around Haunted Towers, Crumbling Castles, and Ghoulish Graveyards* (WordCrafts Press, 2020), as well as the co-editor (with S. T. Joshi) of *The Weird Cat*, an anthology of weird cat stories by writers living and dead (WordCrafts Press, 2023). Her Lovecraftian and Gothic works have been featured in *Black Wings VII*, *Penumbra*, *Journ-E*, *Spectral Realms*, *Illumen*, *Retro-Fan*, *The Little Book of Cursed Dolls* (Media Macabre, 2023), as well as other discerning publications.

Karen Joan Kohoutek, an independent scholar and poet, has published about weird fiction in various journals and literary websites. Recent and upcoming publications have been on subjects including the Gamera films, the Robert E. Howard/H. P. Lovecraft correspondence, folk magic in the novels of Ishmael Reed, and the proto-Gothic writer Charles Brockden Brown. She lives in Fargo, North Dakota.

Michael D. Miller is a former professor of genre studies, currently writing reviews, articles, and poetry for the weird fiction genre with work appearing in *Dead Reckonings, Lovecraft Annual, Spectral Realms, Penumbra, Alien Buddha Press, Dumpster Fire Press,* and *Marchxness*. He is the author of the Realms of Fantasy RPG for Mythopoeia Games Publications.

Daniel Pietersen is the editor of *I Am Stone: The Gothic Weird Tales of R. Murray Gilchrist*, part of the British Library's Tales of the Weird series. He's also a regular contributor to publications like *Revenant* and *Horror Homeroom,* as well as a guest lecturer for the Romancing the Gothic project.

Géza A. G. Reilly is a writer and critic with an interest in twentieth-century American genre literature. A Canadian expatriate, he now lives in the wilds of Florida with his wife, Andrea, and their cat, Mim.

Darrell Schweitzer has been publishing weird or fantastic poetry for decades. Not counting comic verse (e.g., *They Never Found the Head: Poems of Sentiment and Reflection,* 2001) his two previous collections of (mostly weird) verse are *Groping toward the Light* (2000) and *Ghosts of Past and Future* (2008). Hippocampus Press will soon issue a new volume, *Dancing Before Azathoth*, of previously uncollected and selected poems. His most recent story collection is *The Children of Chorazin* (Hippocampus, 2023) and his most recent anthology is *Shadows out of Time* (PS Publishing 2023).

Joe Shea (The joey Zone) is an artist and illustrator. Samples of his work can be found at www.joeyzoneillustration.com.

Taylor Trabulus lives and works in New York City, where she works at a contemporary art gallery. In her free time, she writes horror stories, watches spooky movies, and hangs out with her elderly Chinese Crested dog, Misty.

Josh Yelle is an artist across mediums. His work can generally be found on pencilmancer.com.

www.ingramcontent.com/pod-product-compliance
Lightning Source LLC
Chambersburg PA
CBHW071819020426
42331CB00007B/1550